I Can Learn Age 7-9

MEGA MATHS

Written by Stephen Rutter, Michael Tonge and Rosemary Wise
Illustrated by John Haslam, James Robins and Robins Smythe

About this book

Mega Maths offers practice in numeracy skills as described in the guidelines for the National Numeracy Strategy. The book reflects the content of the National Curriculum in England and Wales and the 5–14 Mathematics programme in Scotland.

The book is divided into five sections. Many skills overlap these divisions. We recommend that your child works through the book in the given order. Repetition and practice will help build skills and confidence.

Answers appear on pages 122–128, so that either you or your child can check and mark the work.

How to help your child

Let your child decide how long he or she wants to work on the book. Give lots of encouragement and praise for effort.

Instructions are written clearly and simply, but you may need to look through the activities and explain what your child is being asked to do. If your child has problems with a type of activity, talk about it together and try to help. You may need to discuss it with your child's class teacher.

About the stickers

Your child can add the 100 fun stickers to the pages of the book, or use them to decorate pencil cases, posters or other items.

About the authors

The authors are teachers and educational consultants with many years' experience in schools.

EGMONT
We bring stories to life

First published in Great Britain in 2002 by Egmont Books Limited,
239 Kensington High Street, London W8 6SA
This edition published 2006
Printed in Italy
ISBN 978 1 4052 2347 2
ISBN 1 4052 2347 8

2 **Contents**

MENTAL MATHS

SHAPES, SPACE and MEASURE

FRACTIONS and DECIMALS

Contents

When you add a small number to a large number, put the large number first. It makes counting on easier!

So $135 + 6 = 141$

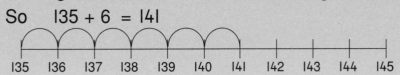

135 136 137 138 139 140 141 142 143 144 145

Top tip:
When you are counting on, count the jumps, not the numbers themselves.

Use the number lines to help you work out these:

$78 + 5 = 83$

77 78 79 80 81 82 83 84 85

$124 + 8 = 132$

124 125 126 127 128 129 130 131 132

$235 + 7 = 242$

235 236 237 238 239 240 241 242 243

$337 + 4 = 341$

337 338 339 340 341 342 343 344 345

You can count on in 10s as well as in 1s:

so $60 + 30 = 90$

50 60 70 80 90 100

and $76 + 50 = 126$

76 86 96 106 116 126

Top tip:
Pick any number you like and count on in 10s – see how far you can get.

Try these:

$85 + 30 = 115$

65 75 85 95 105 115 125

$124 + 40 = 164$

124 134 144 154 164 174 184

$68 + 50 = 118$

68 78 88 98 108 118 128

$95 + 20 = 115$

75 85 95 105 115 125 135

Carry on this pattern:

0,   5,   10,   15,   _20_,   _25_,   _30_,   _35_,   _40_,   _45_

Try counting on in 5s starting from a different number:

8,   13,   18,   23,   28,   33,   _38_,   _43_,   _48_,   _53_

Can you see a pattern?   _+5_

Try these:

6,   11,   16,   21,   _26_,   _31_,   _36_,   _41_,   _46_,   _51_

9,   14,   19,   24,   _29_,   _34_,   _39_,   _44_,   _49_,   _54_

7,   12,   17,   22,   _27_,   _32_,   _37_,   _42_,   _47_,   _52_

When you add several numbers together, look for the pairs that make 10:

4 + 5 + 3 + 6 + 5
= (4 + 6) + (5 + 5) + 3
= 10 + 10 + 3
= 20 + 3 = 23

Top tip:

When you add numbers together you can do it in any order.

Use this method to add these numbers:

3 + 5 + 7 + 5 + 2 = _5 + 5_
_____ _7 + 3_
_____ _2 + 3 + 5_

6 + 3 + 4 + 1 + 7 = _3 + 7_
_____ _4 + 6_
_____ _1 + 3 + 6_

Brain Box

Top tip:

You can add on 10, 20, 30 and so on to any number. Use this knowledge to add numbers like 9, 19 and 29.

First add the multiple of 10 and then subtract 1, like this: $253 + 9 = 253 + 10 - 1 = 263 - 1 = 262$

$342 + 19 = 342 + 20 - 1 = 362 - 1 = 361$

Try to do these sums in your head. You do not need to write down all the steps.

$56 + 9 = \underline{65}$　　　$74 + 19 = \underline{93}$

$87 + 29 = \underline{116}$　　　$63 + 39 = \underline{109}$

$134 + 9 = \underline{143}$　　$236 + 19 = \underline{255}$

$323 + 29 = \underline{342}$　　$354 + 39 = \underline{382}$

You can use a similar method to add 11, 21, 31 and so on.

$76 + 21 = 76 + 20 + 1 = 96 + 1 = 97$
$365 + 31 = 365 + 30 + 1 = 395 + 1 = 396$

Try these:

$85 + 11 = \underline{96}$　　　$64 + 21 = \underline{85}$　　　$58 + 31 = \underline{89}$　　　$72 + 41 = \underline{201}$

$134 + 11 = \underline{154}$　　$435 + 21 = \underline{465}$　　$546 + 31 = \underline{576}$　　$227 + 41 = \underline{258}$

You can adapt this method if you need to subtract.

$87 - 9 = 87 - 10 + 1 = 77 + 1 = 78$
$126 - 11 = 126 - 10 - 1 = 116 - 1 = 115$

Try these:

$76 - 9 = \underline{67}$　　　$86 - 19 = \underline{}$　　　$154 - 29 = \underline{}$　　　$345 - 39 = \underline{}$

$86 - 11 = \underline{}$　　　$93 - 21 = \underline{}$　　　$386 - 31 = \underline{}$　　　$556 - 41 = \underline{}$

Top tip:

Always look for patterns in a series of sums. Patterns will help you to solve other sums of the same type.

Look at the sums below. See if you can spot the pattern and carry it on:

17 + 5 = 22	87 − 4 = 83
17 + 15 = 32	87 − 14 = 73
17 + 25 = 42	87 − 24 = 63
17 + 35 = 52	87 − 34 = 53
17 + 45 = 62	87 − 44 = 43
17 + 55 = 72	87 − 54 = 33
17 + 65 = 82	87 − 64 = 23
17 + 75 = 92	87 − 74 = 13
17 + 85 = 102	87 − 84 = 3

Look for the pattern in these sums and carry it on:

5 +	3 =	8
50 +	30 =	80
500 +	300 =	800
5000 +	3000 =	8000
7 −	2 =	5
70 −	20 =	50
700 −	200 =	500
7000 −	2000 =	5000

See if you can spot the pattern in this addition table and complete it:

+	1	2	3	4	5	6	7	8	9	10
1	2	3	4	5	6	7	8	9	10	11
2	3	4	5	6	7	8	9	10	11	12
3	4	5	6	7	8	9	10	11	12	13
4	5	6	7	8	9	10	11	12	13	14
5	6	7	8	9	10	11	12	13	14	15
6	7	8	9	10	11	12	13	14	15	16
7	8	9	10	11	12	13	14	15	16	17
8	9	10	11	12	13	14	15	16	17	18
9	10	11	12	13	14	15	16	17	18	19
10	11	12	13	14	15	16	17	18	19	20

Cool Kid

There are 5 pirate ships.

There are 7 pirates in each ship.

There are 35 pirates altogether, because 7 x 5 = 35.

35 pirates divided between 5 ships gives 7 pirates on each ship: 35 ÷ 5 = 7.

This shows that multiplication and division are the opposite of each other.

Top tip:

To find the answer to 45 ÷ 5, look in the x5 table until you see the number 45 and you will see that: 9 x 5 = 45 so 45 ÷ 5 = 9

deep thinking

Use the x2, x5 and x10 tables to answer these division sums:

20 ÷ 2 = _____10_____   16 ÷ 2 = _____8_____

40 ÷ 5 = _____8_____   25 ÷ 5 = _____5_____

40 ÷ 10 = _____4_____   60 ÷ 10 = _____6_____

Divide 18 by 2 _____9_____   Divide 14 by 2 _____7_____

Divide 35 by 5 _____7_____   Divide 15 by 5 _____3_____

Divide 50 by 10 _____5_____   Divide 80 by 10 _____8_____

Halving means dividing by 2. When we want to find half of something we divide it by 2.

What is half of 12? _____ 6 _____

What is half of 8? _____ 4 _____

What is half of 20? _____ 10 ✓ _____

Doubling means multiplying by 2.

What is double 6? _____ 12 _____

What is double 4? _____ 8 _____

What is double 10? _____ 20 ✓ _____

Show your workings here:
 Sticker

out of this world

Top tip:

Doubling and halving are the opposite of each other. You can use your multiplication facts to work out sums with bigger numbers.

Carry on counting in 2s to complete this table:

11 x 2 = 22

12 x 2 = 24

13 x 2 = 26

14 x 2 = 28

15 x 2 = 30

16 x 2 = 32

17 x 2 = 34

18 x 2 = 36

19 x 2 = 38

20 x 2 = 40

Can you spot a pattern here and carry it on?

Half of 22 is 11

Half of 24 is 12

Half of 26 is 13

Half of 28 is 14

Half of 30 is 15

Half of 32 is 16 ✓

Half of 34 is 17

Half of 36 is 18

Half of 38 is 19

Half of 40 is 20

How many of these sums can you answer in 5 minutes?

14 + 16 = ___30___ ✓   18 + 22 = ___40___ ✓

35 + 25 = ___60___ ✓   37 + 23 = ___50___

49 + 21 = ___70___ ✓   48 + 22 = ___60___

38 + 32 = ___70___ ✓   57 + 33 = ___80___

63 + 27 = ___90___ ✓   24 + 66 = ___80___

Did you notice anything about all the answers?

Now try again with these. How many can you get right in 5 minutes? You have to fill in the missing numbers:

95 + ___5___ = 100   23 + _____ = 100

60 + ___40___ = 100   98 + _____ = 100

20 + ___80___ = 100   88 + _____ = 100

59 + ___40___ = 100   51 + _____ = 100

40 + ___60___ = 100   48 + _____ = 100

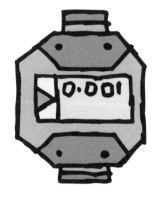

Top tip:

It is important to be able to work quickly when you want to. The more you practise the quicker you will get. But no matter how quick you are, it only counts if the answers are right.

Beat the clock

See how many of these you can do in 5 minutes:

8 x 2 = _16_   45 ÷ 5 = _9_

6 x 5 = _30_   18 ÷ 2 = _9_

9 x 10 = _40_   50 ÷ 10 = _5_

5 x 3 = _15_   25 ÷ 5 = _5_

2 x 7 = _14_   60 ÷ 10 = _6_

Show your ~~workings~~ here:
sticker

Great idea!

Now try these.
How quickly can you answer them?

23 x 10 = _230_   350 ÷ 10 = _35_

25 x 2 = _50_   34 ÷ 2 = _16_

30 x 10 = _300_   100 ÷ 2 = _200_

14 x 2 = _28_   650 ÷ 10 = _65_

3 x 100 = _300_   700 ÷ 100 = _7_

You must be able to add together any two numbers up to 20 + 20, and subtract from any number up to 20. These are the number facts up to 20.

Decode this secret message by finding the answers and then filling in the letters.

5 + 7	20 − 15	18 − 17	9 + 9	6 + 8	20 − 11	7 + 7	20 − 13
12	5	1	18	14	9	14	7

11 + 9	12 − 4	15 − 10	11 + 8	14 − 9
20	8	5	19	5

14 − 8	18 − 17	12 − 9	3 + 17	12 + 7
6	1	3	14	19

14 − 6	17 − 12	17 − 5	13 + 3	14 + 5
8	5			

11 + 9	18 − 3

6 + 13	9 + 6	20 − 8	11 + 11	19 − 14

15 − 7	13 − 12	9 + 9	16 − 12	19 − 14	10 + 8

5 + 11	20 − 2	20 − 5	11 − 9	5 + 7	13 − 8	20 − 7	6 + 13

A	B	C	D	E	F	G	H	I	J	K	L	M
1	2	3	4	5	6	7	8	9	10	11	12	13

N	O	P	Q	R		U	V	W	X	Y	Z
14	15	16	17	18	19	21	22	23	24	25	26

Use your knowledge of number pairs to add up and subtract multiples of 10 and 100.

If 5 + 7 = 12   then 50 + 70 = 120   and 500 + 700 = 1200
if 8 − 3 = 5   then 80 − 30 = 50   and 800 − 300 = 500

Write down the answers to these:

40 +   30 = _____   50 +   90 = _____   60 +   70 = _____   70 +   80 = _____

500 + 600 = _____   600 + 900 = _____   800 + 400 = _____   400 + 300 = _____

60 −   10 = _____   90 −   30 = _____   80 −   40 = _____   100 −   30 = _____

600 − 400 = _____   1200 − 300 = _____   700 − 100 = _____   1500 − 800 = _____

The numbers on the explorers are the answers to the sums on the boats.
Draw lines to join each explorer to the correct boat:

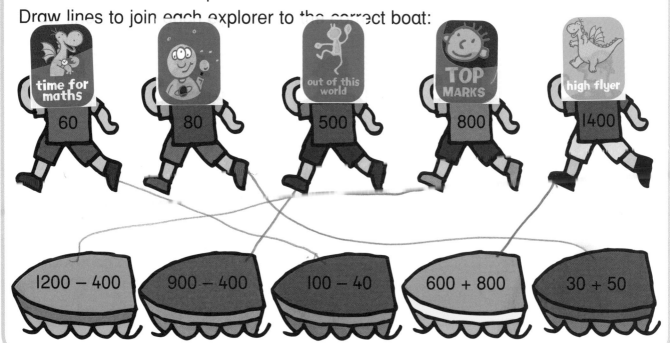

Number pairs

You need to be able to recognise the pairs of numbers that make 100.

First try some number pairs that make 10.
Draw a ring round the pairs that make 10:

3 + 7   4 + 8   6 + 5   6 + 4   5 + 5   7 + 4   2 + 8

Now draw rings round the pairs that make 100.

40 + 60   50 + 70   20 + 80

30 + 80   50 + 60   30 + 70

90 + 10   70 + 50   80 + 30

Now you can try some harder ones.
Draw rings round the 100 pairs:

38 + 62   45 + 65   18 + 82

53 + 47   24 + 76   67 + 45

65 + 45   74 + 28   74 + 25

Top tip:

Look at the units first – do they make 10? Then look to see if the tens add up to the remaining 90.
64 + 36 = 100 because 4 + 6 = 10
60 + 30 = 90 and 10 + 90 = 100

I wrote out lots of number pairs on bits of paper but someone tore them up.
Can you draw lines to show which bit of paper goes with which to make 100?

45 +   56 +   37 +   81 +   46 +   34 +   71 +

 63   19   55   44   29   66   54

If you know the number pairs that make 100,
it is easy to find the pairs that make 1000.

If 60 + 40 = 100   then   600 + 400 = 1000

If 45 + 55 = 100   then   450 + 550 = 1000

Next to each number, write down the
number that would make it up to 1000:

500 _500_   700 _300_   200 _800_

950 _50_   750 _350_   650 _450_

Colour in the multiples of 5 to find the hidden number.

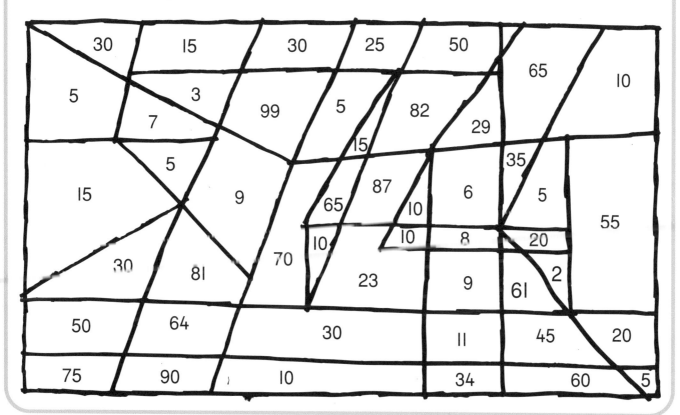

When you have to add a lot of numbers together, remember you can do it in any order.
It helps if you can find pairs of numbers.

$2 + 5 + 9 + 5 + 3 + 1 + 8$ is easier if you do

$2 + 8 = 10$ → $5 + 5 = 10$ → $9 + 1 = 10$ →

$10 + 10 + 10 = 30$ → $30 + 3 = 33$

Show your workings here:

sticker

Look for pairs that make 20 or 100:

$17 + 8 + 12 + 3 = (17 + 3) + (8 + 12) = 20 + 20 = 40$

You will not always find easy pairs. Then it is usually best to start with the large numbers and then add the smaller ones:

So $5 + 17 + 7 + 20$ is easier if you do it in the order:

$20 + 17 = 37$

$37 + 7 = 44$

$44 + 5 = 49$

Time yourself and see how quickly you can add these up:

$2 + 5 + 8 + 5 =$ _____ $17 + 5 + 3 + 25 =$ _____

$60 + 20 + 40 + 80 =$ _____ $18 + 70 + 2 + 30 =$ _____

$9 + 24 + 5 + 13 =$ _____ $5 + 32 + 23 + 7 =$ _____

$13 + 5 + 7 + 60 + 4 + 6 + 5 =$ _____

Pairing and sharing

To share 31 sweets between 5 people, you can give 6 sweets to each person (5 x 6 = 30), but there is 1 sweet left over.
We say that there is a remainder of 1.

31 ÷ 5 = 6 remainder 1   5 x 6 = 30   31 − 30 = 1

or, for short, we write:

31 ÷ 5 = 6 r 1

Try these:

23 ÷ 2 = _____ r _____   15 ÷ 2 = _____ r _____   13 ÷ 2 = _____ r _____

27 ÷ 2 = _____ r _____   34 ÷ 5 = _____ r _____   43 ÷ 5 = _____ r _____

12 children want to play five-a-side football.
How many teams will there be? How many children will be left out?

_____ teams   _____ children left over

32 eggs are packed in boxes of 6.
How many full boxes would there be?
How many eggs would be left over?

_____ boxes   _____ eggs left over

45 bottles are packed in crates of 10.
How many crates would there be?
How many bottles would be left over?

_____ crates   _____ bottles left over

I have £5 to share between 4 people:

  £5 ÷ 4 = £1 remainder £1

but we can turn the remaining pound into 100p and share that out:

100p ÷ 4 = 25p

so each person ends up with £1 and 25p = £1.25

  £5 ÷ 4 = £1.25

Try these:

  £7 ÷ 2 = £ _____   £9 ÷ 2 = £ _____   £5 ÷ 2 = £ _____

  £9 ÷ 4 = £ _____   £14 ÷ 4 = £ _____   £17 ÷ 4 = £ _____

  £16 ÷ 5 = £ _____   £32 ÷ 5 = £ _____   £39 ÷ 4 = £ _____

  £32 ÷ 10 = £ _____   £43 ÷ 10 = £ _____   £64 ÷ 10 = £ _____

5 children want to buy a football between them which costs £16.

How much will each child have to pay? _____

---

4 people buy a winning ticket for the lottery.
They win £10 between them.
How much will each person get? _____

Mary saves up for 10 weeks to buy a pair of shoes.
The shoes cost £25.
How much must she save each week? _____

Do you know your x3 and x4 tables?

Add on in 4s to complete this x4 table:

0 x 4 = 0

1 x 4 = 4

2 x 4 = 8

3 x 4 = 12

4 x 4 = _____

5 x 4 = _____

6 x 4 = _____

7 x 4 = _____

8 x 4 = _____

9 x 4 = _____

10 x 4 = _____

Add on in 3s to complete this x3 table:

0 x 3 = 0

1 x 3 = 3

2 x 3 = 6

3 x 3 = 9

4 x 3 = _____

5 x 3 = _____

6 x 3 = _____

7 x 3 = _____

8 x 3 = _____

9 x 3 = _____

10 x 3 = _____

Top tip:

You need to practise saying your tables until you know them by heart. Remember that multiplication can be done either way round. So when you learn that 6 x 3 = 18 you also know that 3 x 6 = 18!

A group of four explorers have found an ancient tomb.
To open the door they must press the right buttons.

Help the explorers open the door by marking the right buttons with a tick.

To find the right buttons, answer these sums:

7 x 2 =_____

6 x 3 =_____

8 x 4 =_____

10 x 5 =_____

9 x 10 =_____

When the explorers get through the door, they see an old chest.

To open the chest they must find the right key.

The key to open the chest is in the x3 and x5 tables but not in the x2, x4 or x10 tables.

Which key do they pick?

In the chest the explorers find an old piece of paper. On it is a message in code. Can you solve the puzzle and decode the message?

$$\frac{7 \times 4}{4 \times 7} \quad \frac{3 \times 3}{5 \times 5} \quad \frac{1 \times 5}{1 \times 5} \quad \frac{0 \times 3}{\rule{1cm}{0.4pt}} \quad \frac{9 \times 3}{\rule{1cm}{0.4pt}} \quad \frac{10 \times 3}{\rule{1cm}{0.4pt}} \quad \frac{5 \times 5}{\rule{1cm}{0.4pt}} \quad \frac{5 \times 1}{\rule{1cm}{0.4pt}}$$

$$\frac{5 \times 2}{3 \times 3} \quad \frac{3 \times 9}{2 \times 5} \quad \frac{4 \times 1}{6 \times 5} \quad \frac{2 \times 2}{5 \times 5} \quad \frac{1 \times 5}{\rule{1cm}{0.4pt}} \quad \frac{6 \times 3}{\rule{1cm}{0.4pt}}$$

$$\frac{2 \times 3}{7 \times 4} \quad \frac{4 \times 5}{5 \times 2} \quad \frac{6 \times 5}{4 \times 4} \quad \frac{5 \times 5}{5 \times 1} \quad \frac{3 \times 9}{\rule{1cm}{0.4pt}}$$

$$\frac{9 \times 3}{7 \times 3} \quad \frac{10 \times 1}{4 \times 0} \quad \frac{8 \times 5}{3 \times 1} \quad \frac{1 \times 5}{\rule{1cm}{0.4pt}} \quad \frac{3 \times 9}{\rule{1cm}{0.4pt}}$$

$$\frac{6 \times 3}{2 \times 10} \quad \frac{5 \times 4}{6 \times 1} \quad \frac{5 \times 5}{\rule{1cm}{0.4pt}} \quad \frac{4 \times 7}{\rule{1cm}{0.4pt}} \quad \frac{3 \times 3}{\rule{1cm}{0.4pt}}$$

$$\frac{7 \times 4}{5 \times 4} \quad \frac{1 \times 9}{5 \times 3} \quad \frac{5 \times 1}{2 \times 2}$$

$$\frac{9 \times 3}{\rule{1cm}{0.4pt}} \quad \frac{4 \times 7}{\rule{1cm}{0.4pt}} \quad \frac{0 \times 5}{\rule{1cm}{0.4pt}} \quad \frac{14 \times 2}{\rule{1cm}{0.4pt}} \quad \frac{6 \times 5}{\rule{1cm}{0.4pt}} \quad \frac{1 \times 5}{\rule{1cm}{0.4pt}}$$

A	B	C	D	E	F	G	H	I	J	K	L	M
0	2	3	4	5	6	8	9	10	12	14	15	16

N	O	P	Q	R	S	T	U	V	W	X	Y	Z
18	20	21	24	25	27	28	30	32	35	40	45	50

Top tip:

You can use your knowledge of the x2, x3, x4, x5 and x10 tables to do other multiplications.

Show your workings here:

To multiply 2 by 6, multiply by 3 and then by 2.

2 x 6   x 3   6   x 2   12

To multiply by 11, multiply by 10 and then add the number on.

Complete this pattern:

3 x 6   x 3   __9__   x 2   __18__

4 x 6   x 3   _____   x 2   _____

5 x 6   x 3   _____   x 2   _____

6 x 6   x 3   _____   x 2   _____

7 x 6   x 3   _____   x 2   _____

8 x 6   x 3   _____   x 2   _____

9 x 6   x 3   _____   x 2   _____

10 x 6   x 3   _____   x 2   _____

Complete this pattern:

3 x 11   __30 + 3 =__   33

4 x 11   __40 + 4 =__   44

12 x 11   __120 + 12 =__   132

6 x 11   _____

9 x 11   _____

11 x 11   _____

14 x 11   _____

15 x 11   _____

20 x 11   _____

19 x 11   _____

If you want to multiply by 9 there are two ways you can do it.

1. Multiply by 3 and then by 3 again.

8 x 9	8 x 3 = 24	24 x 3 = 72
12 x 9	12 x 3 = 36	36 x 3 = 108

2. Multiply by 10 and then subtract the number.

8 x 9	8 x 10 = 80	80 − 8 = 72
12 x 9	12 x 10 = 120	120 − 12 = 108

Use the first method to calculate:

6 x 9 = _____

7 x 9 = _____

9 x 9 = _____

11 x 9 = _____

15 x 9 = _____

20 x 9 = _____

25 x 9 = _____

Now try the second method:

6 x 9 = _____

7 x 9 = _____

9 x 9 = _____

11 x 9 = _____

15 x 9 = _____

20 x 9 = _____

25 x 9 = _____

Did you get the same answers both times?

Which method do you like best?

Complete the patterns below:

10 x 10 = 100

11 x 10 = 110

12 x 10 = 120

13 x 10 = _____

14 x 10 = _____

15 x 10 = _____

16 x 10 = _____

17 x 10 = _____

18 x 10 = _____

19 x 10 = _____

20 x 10 = _____

30 x 10 =   300

35 x 10 =   350

40 x 10 = _____

45 x 10 = _____

50 x 10 = _____

55 x 10 = _____

60 x 10 = _____

65 x 10 = _____

70 x 10 = _____

75 x 10 = _____

80 x 10 = _____

Mercury bars are packed in boxes of 10.
How many bars are there in:

32 boxes? _____   24 boxes?_____   48 boxes?_____

53 boxes? _____   135 boxes?_____   246 boxes?_____

The delivery lorries can carry 100 boxes each.
How many boxes are there in:

8 lorries? _____   15 lorries?_____   23 lorries?_____

54 lorries? _____   68 lorries?_____   125 lorries?_____

Show your
workings here:

How many boxes would you need for:

50 bars?   ÷ 10   =   5 boxes

120 bars?   ÷ 10   =   12 boxes

380 bars?   _____

470 bars?   _____

1560 bars?   _____

2600 bars?   _____

How many lorries would you need to carry:

300 boxes?   ÷ 100   =   3 lorries

4500 boxes?   ÷ 100   =   45 lorries

3800 boxes?   _____

2900 boxes?   _____

8600 boxes?   _____

10 000 boxes? _____

You can check any subtraction by changing the sum into an addition and seeing if you get the number you started with.

$336 - 52 = 284$ check $284 + 52 = 336$

Top tip:

Sometimes it is a good idea to check your answers.

You can also use multiplication to check divisions:

$$120 \div 4 = 30$$
check $30 \times 4 = 120$

Mary did some subtractions. Use an addition to check whether she got them right. Put a tick by the ones she got right and a cross by the ones she got wrong.

$425 - 38 = 387$ _____

$347 - 85 = 262$ _____

$235 - 57 = 176$ _____

$118 - 63 = 45$ _____

$531 - 143 = 388$ _____

Jacob did some divisions. Check his answers by doing a multiplication. Be careful – he got some wrong!

Tick the right divisions and put a cross by the wrong ones.

$350 \div 5 = 70$ _____

$84 \div 4 = 22$ _____

$156 \div 3 = 52$ _____

$164 \div 4 = 41$ _____

$225 \div 5 = 44$ _____

Another way to check your calculations is to make an estimate to see if you are about right.

38 + 47 = 85	estimate	40 + 50 = 90	about right
713 − 68 = 145	estimate	700 − 70 = 630	must be wrong
38 x 9 = 214	estimate	40 x 10 = 400	must be wrong
963 − 9 = 954	estimate	1000 − 10 = 900	about right

Use an estimate to check these calculations and put a cross by the ones you think are wrong:

67 + 198 = 355 _____

651 − 49 = 202 _____

52 x 11 = 572 _____

486 − 9 = 540 _____

Show your workings here:

Top tip:

If you add even numbers together, the answer is always even.

16	+	18	+	12	=	46
even		even		even		even

Put a cross by the sums you think are wrong:

6 + 12 + 18 = 38 _____   14 + 24 + 32 + 16 = 86 _____

24 + 30 + 16 = 83 _____   246 + 348 = 594 _____

56 + 38 = 121 _____   356 + 462 = 889 _____

This shape has a line of symmetry marked down the middle.

A line of symmetry is like a mirror image line.

One side of the line of symmetry is an exact mirror image of the other.

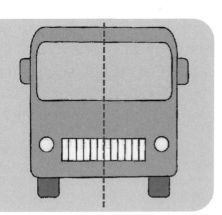

Complete these shapes where the line of symmetry is marked:

Now mark the line of symmetry on these shapes:

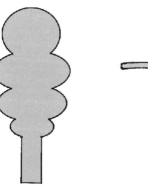
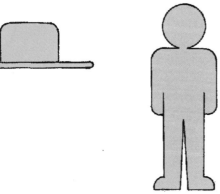

Many shapes have more
than one line of symmetry.
This butterfly has two.

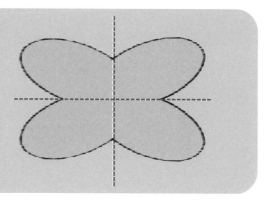

Complete these shapes so they each have more than one line of symmetry.
The lines of symmetry are marked on the pictures.

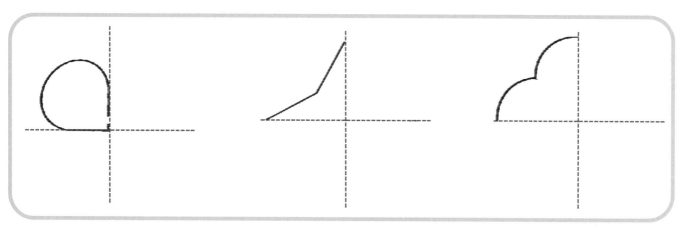

How many lines of symmetry does each shape have?

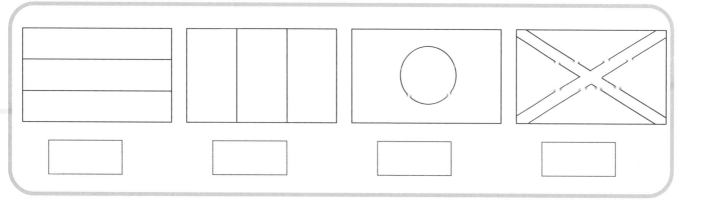

An angle is the space between two lines. Put these angles in the correct order. Start with the smallest.

Top tip:
Use the corner of a piece of paper to help you, or trace the angles and compare them on paper.

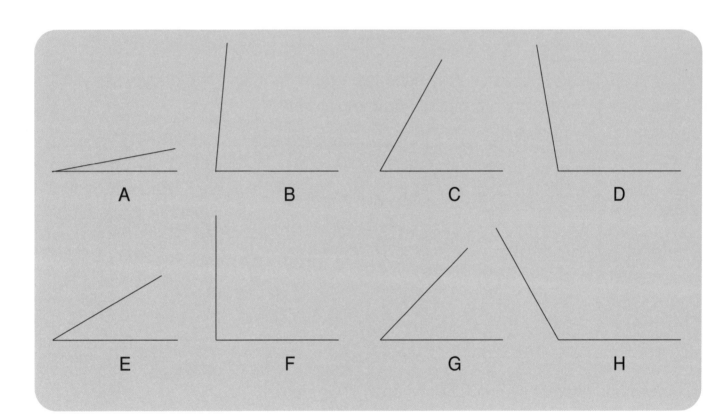

A   B   C   D

E   F   G   H

The correct order is:

_____

A right angle is a quarter turn. This is a right angle: ⌐

This angle is bigger than a right angle: ＼_

This angle is smaller than a right angle: ∠

For each shape, answer these questions:

1. What is its name?
2. How many sides does it have?
3. How many right angles does it have?
4. How many angles are larger than a right angle?
5. How many angles are smaller than a right angle?
6. How many vertices are there?

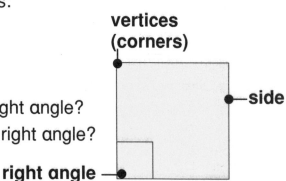

1._____
2._____   3._____
4._____   5._____   6._____

1._____
2._____   3._____
4._____   5._____   6._____

1._____
2._____   3._____
4._____   5._____   6._____

1._____
2._____   3._____
4._____   5._____   6._____

1._____
2._____   3._____
4._____   5._____   6._____ __

1._____
2._____   3._____
4._____   5._____   6._____

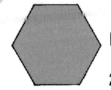

1._____
2._____   3._____
4._____   5._____   6._____

1._____
2._____   3._____
4._____   5._____   6._____

Write the letter of each shape alongside
the correct name in the table below.

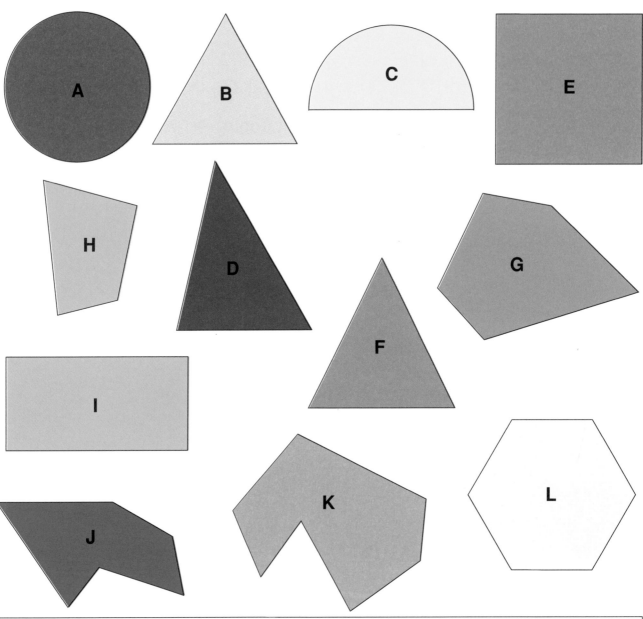

Names				
isosceles triangle		rectangle	circle	hexagon	
triangle		semi-circle	regular hexagon	square	
equilateral triangle		pentagon	quadrilateral	heptagon	

Fill in the number of faces, edges
and vertices for each of the shapes below.

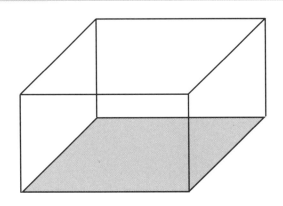

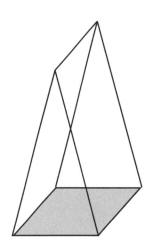

Cuboid

Faces _____

Edges _____

Vertices _____

Triangular Prism

Faces _____

Edges _____

Vertices _____

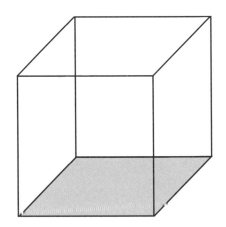

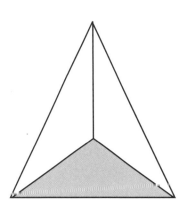

Cube

Faces _____

Edges _____

Vertices _____

Tetrahedron

Faces _____

Edges _____

Vertices _____

The perimeter is the total distance around a shape.

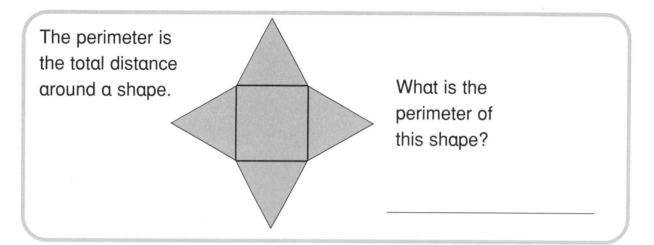

What is the perimeter of this shape?

_____

A regular octagon has sides that measure 3cm each.

What is its perimeter? _____

Which is bigger: a hexagon where each side measures 3cm,

or a square where side measures 4cm? _____

Draw four shapes on the grid below:
 perimeter = 8cm   perimeter = 12cm
 perimeter = 4cm   perimeter = 10cm

To calculate the area of a shape we multiply its length by its breadth.

3 centimetre squares x 2 centimetre squares = 6 centimetre squares.

We write this as 6cm^2.

Measure the length and breadth of each shape. Then calculate the area of each shape.

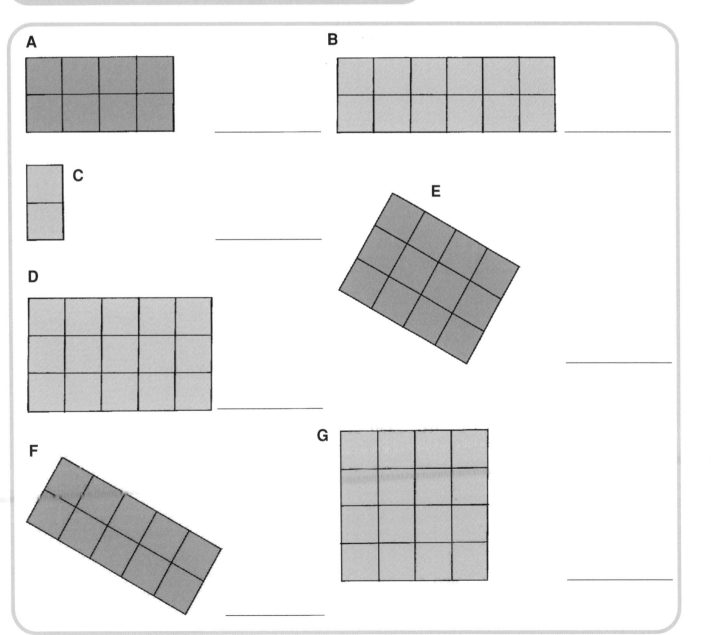

A

B

_____

_____

C

_____

E

D

_____

_____

G

F

_____

_____

Measure and calculate the perimeter and area of these rectangles.

A

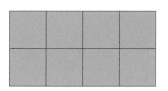

perimeter = _____

area   = _____

B

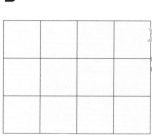

Top tip:

The **perimeter** is the distanc[e] around a shape. The **area** i[s] the space inside a shape, always noted with ^{2} after th[e] unit of measurement.

perimeter = _____

area   = _____

C

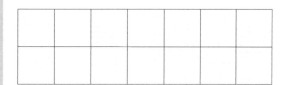

perimeter = _____

area   = _____

D

perimeter = _____

area   = _____

E

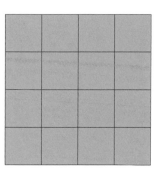

perimeter = _____

area   = _____

F

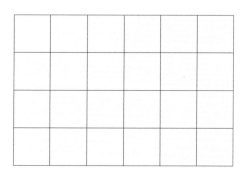

perimeter = _____

area   = _____

Measure and calculate the perimeter and area of these shapes.

A

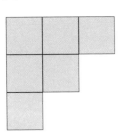

perimeter = _____

area   = _____

B

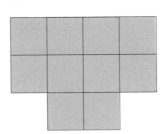

perimeter = _____

area   = _____

C

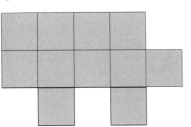

perimeter = _____

area   = _____

D

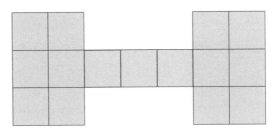

perimeter = _____

area   = _____

E

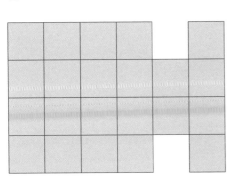

perimeter = _____

area   = _____

F

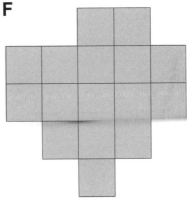

perimeter = _____

area   = _____

We calculate the volume of an object by multiplying its length by its height and then by its width.

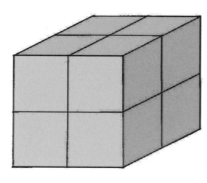

What is the volume of this object? Volume is noted with ^{3} after the unit of measurement

_____

This shape is 2cm long, 2cm high and 2cm wide.
2cm x 2cm x 2cm = 8cm^3

Calculate the volume of these objects.
They are not drawn to scale.

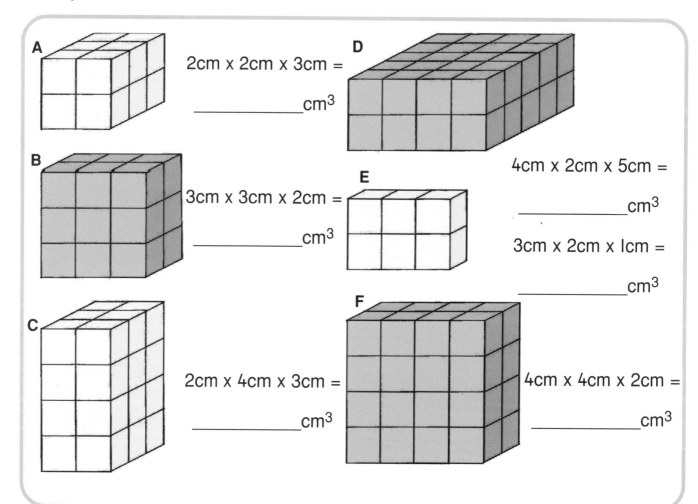

A

2cm x 2cm x 3cm =

_____cm^3

D

4cm x 2cm x 5cm =

_____cm^3

B

3cm x 3cm x 2cm =

_____cm^3

E

3cm x 2cm x 1cm =

_____cm^3

C

2cm x 4cm x 3cm =

_____cm^3

F

4cm x 4cm x 2cm =

_____cm^3

This cube has a volume of $1cm^3$.

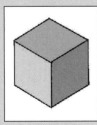

What is the volume of this shape? **A**

_____ cm^3

Work out the volumes of these irregular shapes.
They are all made from centimetre cubes.

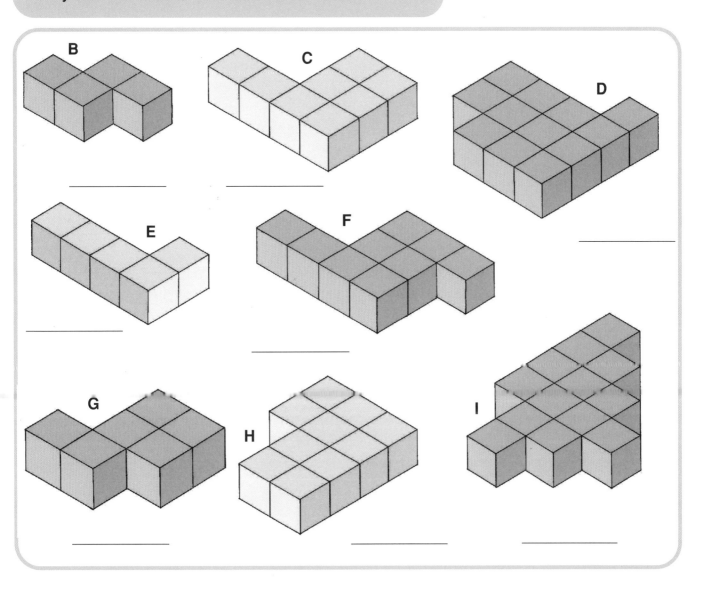

B _____

C _____

D _____

E _____

F _____

G _____

H _____

I _____

Choose from the list below, to show which instrument
and unit you would use to measure each object.

Object	Instrument	Unit
	measuring jug	ml
	ruler	cm
	scales	g
	tape measure	m
	foot measure	

1

Coffee in a mug   _____   _____

2

Length of a foot   _____   _____

3

Weight of an apple   _____   _____

4

Length of a scarf   _____   _____

Measuring

Top tip:

Remember to use metric units, i.e. kilometres not miles.

Write down the units you would use to measure:

The distance from Liverpool to Manchester _____

The height of a giraffe _____

The weight of a baby _____

The weight of a potato _____

The fizzy orange drink in a can _____

The weight of a packet of crisps _____

The length of a pencil _____

The thickness of a book _____

The amount of lemonade in a large bottle _____

The thickness of a coin _____

How many centimetres are there in a metre? _____

10cm is $\frac{1}{10}$ of a metre. We can write $\frac{1}{10}$ of a metre like this: 0.10m.

How many centimetres are there in half a metre? _____

We can write this as 0.50m.

How many centimetres are there in these metre measurements?

   0.75m   0.38m   1.34m   1.54m   0.98m

_____ _____ _____ _____ _____

We can write 132cm as 1.32m.
Write out these centimetre measurements in metres:

   142cm   154cm   198cm   98cm   134cm

_____ _____ _____ _____ _____

Colour in the lengths that are equal with the same colour.

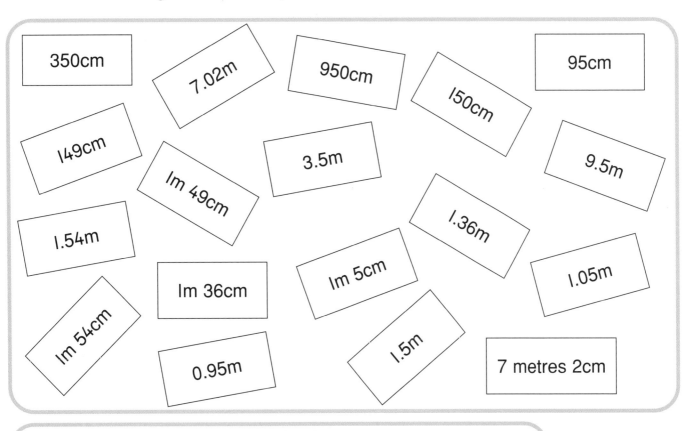

350cm

7.02m

950cm

150cm

95cm

149cm

3.5m

9.5m

1m 49cm

1.54m

1.36m

1m 36cm

1m 5cm

1.05m

1m 54cm

0.95m

1.5m

7 metres 2cm

Now write each pair next to each other.

_____   _____

_____   _____

_____   _____

_____   _____

_____   _____

_____   _____

_____   _____

How much liquid is there in each measuring cylinder?

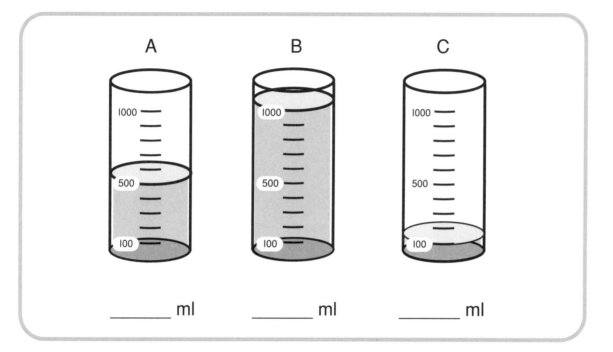

A _____ ml   B _____ ml   C _____ ml

Which cylinder has the greatest amount of liquid? _____

Which cylinder has the least amount of liquid? _____

Look at the cylinders below carefully.
How much liquid does each cylinder contain?

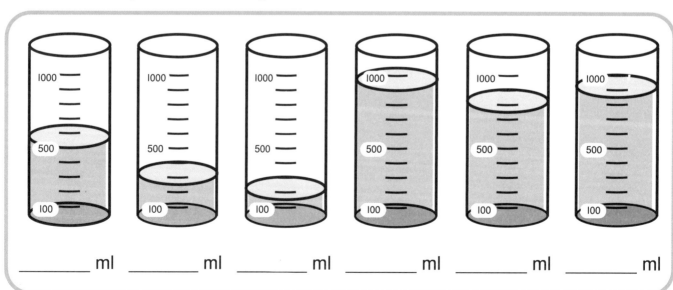

_____ ml _____ ml _____ ml _____ ml _____ ml _____ ml

How much does each parcel weigh?

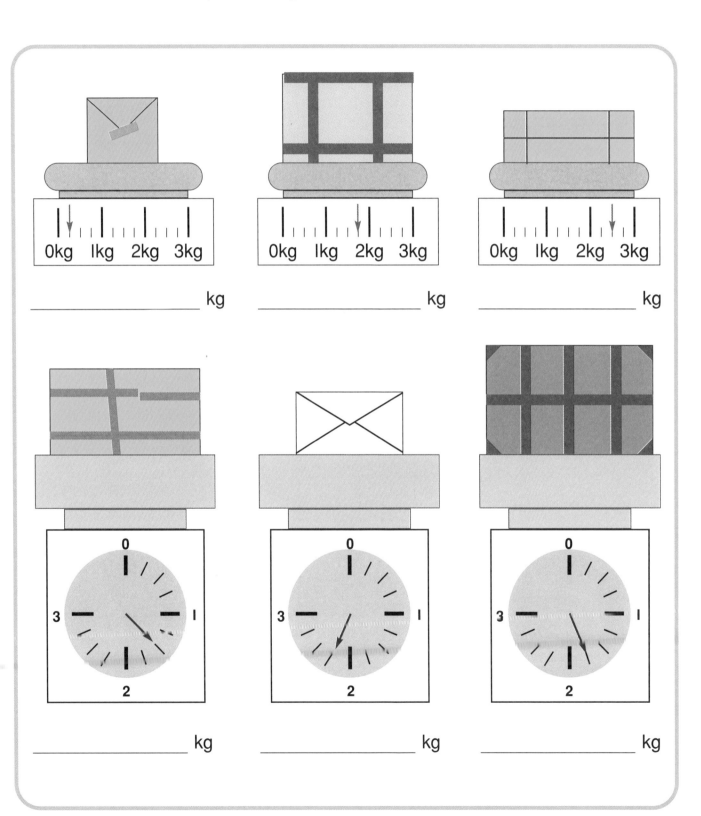

_____ kg   _____ kg   _____ kg

_____ kg   _____ kg   _____ kg

Read the scales and write the answers in each box.

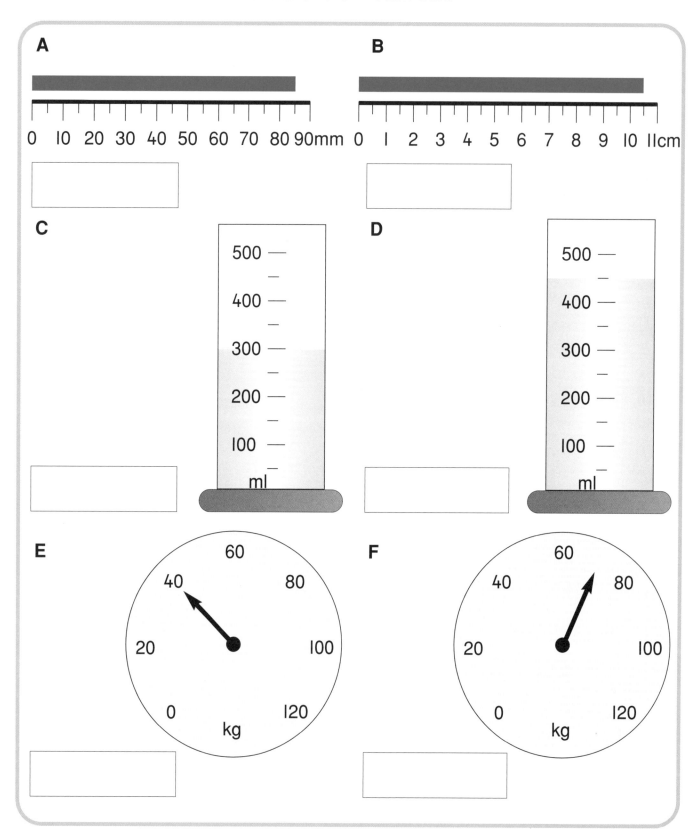

Reading scales

Round each measurement to the nearest unit.

A

Round to the nearest 10cm	
342cm	_____cm
152cm	_____cm
428cm	_____cm
337cm	_____cm

B

Round to the nearest 10cm	
53cm	_____cm
7cm	_____cm
603cm	_____cm
598cm	_____cm

C

Round to the nearest 100 grams	
238g	_____g
1178g	_____g
4640g	_____g
5788g	_____g

D

Round to the nearest 100 grams	
78g	_____g
29g	_____g
4287g	_____g
994g	_____g

Top tip:

When rounding to the nearest 10, we round up when the end digit is more than 5, and round down when it is less than 5.

When rounding to the nearest 100, we check to see if the end digits are more or less than 50.

Here is a piece of a calendar:

NOVEMBER 2003

Sun	Mon	Tue	Wed	Thu	Fri	Sat
	1	2	3	4	5	6
7	8	9	10	11	12	13
14	15	16	17	18	19	20
21	22	23	24	25	26	27
28	29	30				

What day is the third of November? _____

What is the date a fortnight after that? _____

Today is the 17/11/03. Is the day before
it a week day or not? _____

What is the date a week after
the Monday 29th November? _____

If today is the last day of November, how many
days will I have to wait until Christmas day? _____

What date is three weeks before
Sunday 14 November? _____

Read this TV listing:

CHANNEL I		Channel 2		FILM CHANNEL *(new film every 2 hours)*
4:00	ANIMAL SPECIAL	3:55	Ward 7	**Revenge of the Turtle** *(89 mins)*
4:25	CARTOON MYSTERY	4:35	News	_____ _____
		4:45	Madcaps	**Haunted Castle IV** *(118 mins)*
4.50	HERO!	4:50	Junior Art	_____ _____
___	MONSTER TRUCKS	___	Aussie Street	**Mad for Maths III** *(75 mins)*
				_____ _____

Hero! lasts half an hour.
What time does *Monster Trucks* start? _____ Now write it on the page.

Junior Art lasts for three quarters of an hour.
What time does *Aussie Street* begin? _____ Now write it on the page.

How long does *Ward 7* last? _____

How much longer does *Cartoon Mystery*
last than the *News*? _____

Next week there is a two-hour episode of *Animal Special*.
How many more minutes is this than the normal programme? _____

A film begins every two hours on the film channel.
The films start at 4:00.

Write the time each film starts and finishes on the listing at the top of the page.

Reflect the shape in the dotted line.

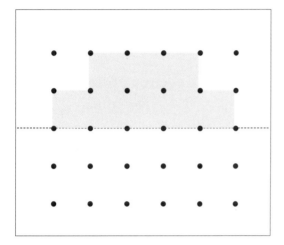

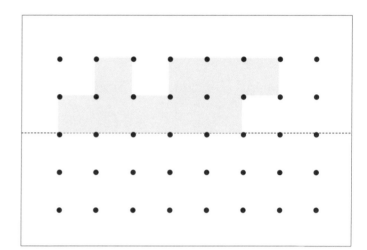

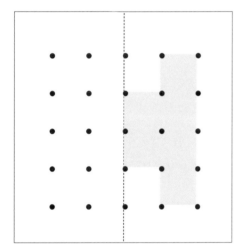

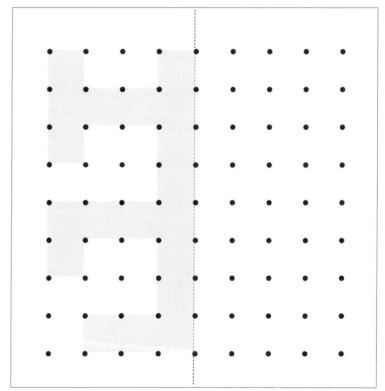

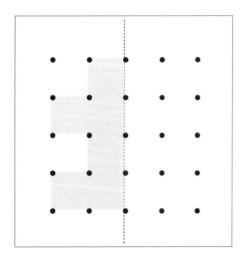

Now reflect each of these shapes in the dotted line.

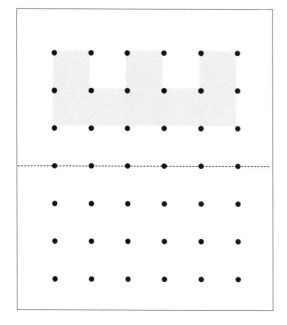

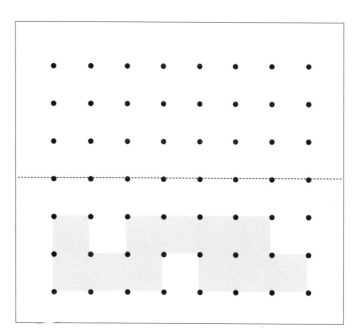

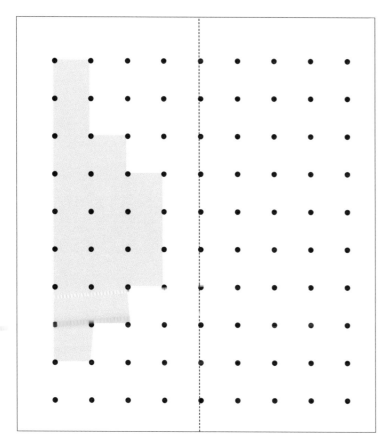

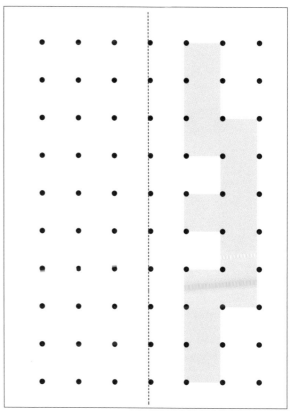

How much of each shape is coloured in?
Use the words and fractions at the bottom of the
page to fill in the spaces under each shape.

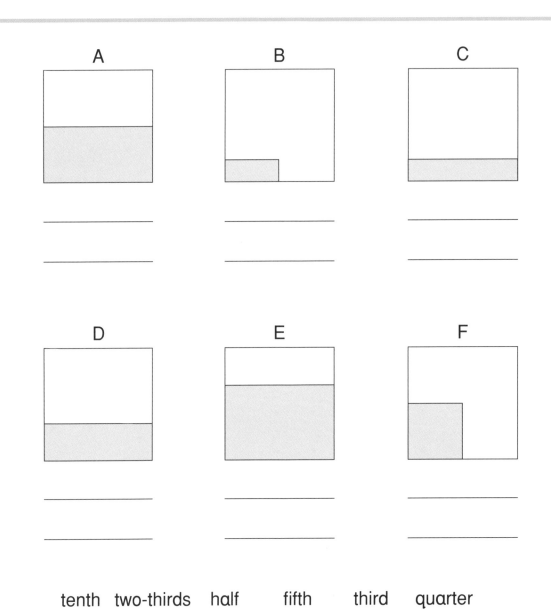

tenth   two-thirds   half   fifth   third   quarter

$\frac{1}{2}$ $\frac{1}{10}$ $\frac{1}{5}$ $\frac{1}{3}$ $\frac{2}{3}$ $\frac{1}{4}$

Colour in each shape to match the amount written underneath.

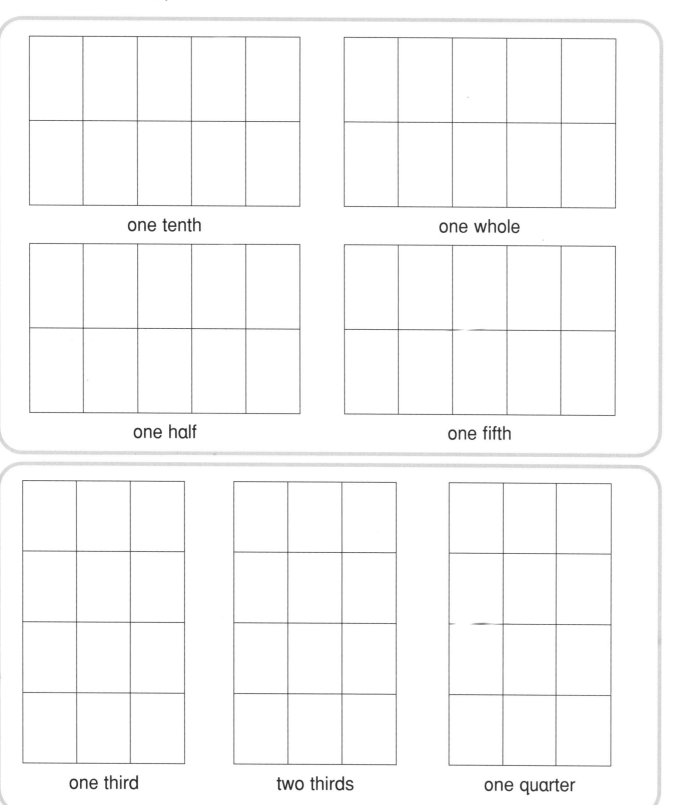

one tenth

one whole

one half

one fifth

one third

two thirds

one quarter

Look at these boxes of chocolates. Some have been eaten.

What fraction of each box of chocolates *hasn't* been eaten?

Example: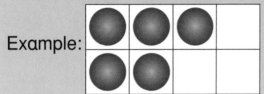

answer: $\frac{5}{8}$ number of chocolates left / number of chocolates when full

A

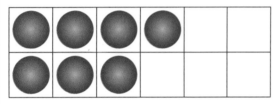

———

B

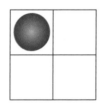

———

C

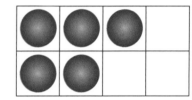

———

D

———

E

———

F

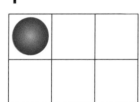

———

G

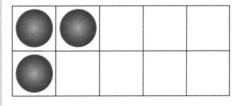

———

H

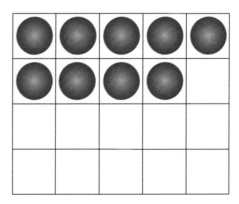

———

Draw the chocolates that are left in the box.
The fraction is written below the box.

Example:

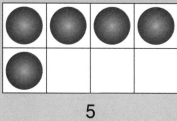

$$\frac{5}{8}$$

A

$$\frac{7}{10}$$

B

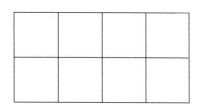

$$\frac{3}{8}$$

C

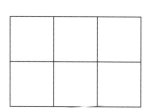

$$\frac{5}{6}$$

D

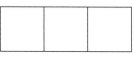

$$\frac{2}{3}$$

E

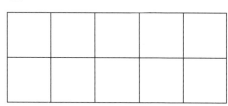

$$\frac{9}{10}$$

F

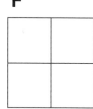

$$\frac{3}{4}$$

G

$$\frac{13}{20}$$

H

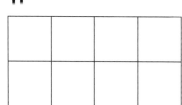

$$\frac{7}{8}$$

Calculate how many buttons should be circled for each amount.
Then complete the number problem.

Circle half the buttons.

$\frac{1}{2}$ of 10 equals _____

Circle a quarter of the buttons.

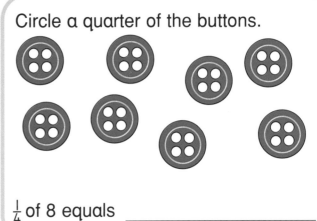

$\frac{1}{4}$ of 8 equals _____

Circle a tenth of the buttons.

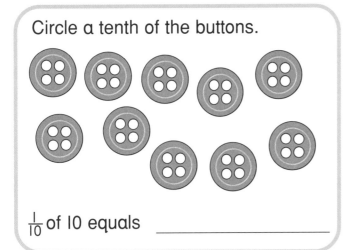

$\frac{1}{10}$ of 10 equals _____

Circle a third of the buttons.

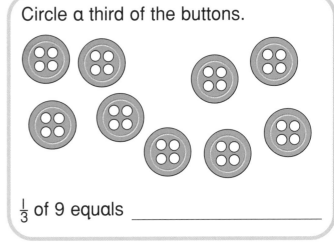

$\frac{1}{3}$ of 9 equals _____

Complete these sentences:

To find half of a number you divide by _____

To find a third of a number you divide by _____

To find a quarter of a number you divide by _____

To find a tenth of a number you divide by _____

> Remember:
>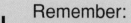
> The top part of a fraction tells us how many pieces we have.
> The bottom part of a fraction tells us how many pieces the whole has been divided into.
> $\frac{2}{3}$ means the whole number has been cut into 3 pieces and we have 2 of them.

Write how many each circle has been cut into, and how many pieces we have:

$\frac{1}{2}$ The circle has been cut into _____ pieces.

We have _____ of them.

$\frac{1}{3}$ The circle has been cut into _____ pieces.

We have _____ of them.

$\frac{1}{4}$ The circle has been cut into _____ pieces.

We have _____ of them.

$\frac{2}{3}$ The circle has been cut into _____ pieces.

We have _____ of them.

$\frac{3}{4}$ The circle has been cut into _____ pieces.

We have _____ of them.

Join the fractions which add up to 1.
The first one is done for you.

A

$\dfrac{1}{4}$ $\qquad$ $\dfrac{2}{3}$

$\dfrac{1}{6}$ $\qquad$ $\dfrac{7}{8}$

$\dfrac{1}{2}$ $\qquad$ $\dfrac{4}{5}$

$\dfrac{1}{3}$ $\qquad$ $\dfrac{1}{2}$

$\dfrac{1}{5}$ $\qquad$ $\dfrac{3}{4}$

$\dfrac{1}{8}$ $\qquad$ $\dfrac{5}{6}$

B

$\dfrac{3}{10}$ $\qquad$ $\dfrac{3}{5}$

$\dfrac{5}{8}$ $\qquad$ $\dfrac{5}{9}$

$\dfrac{2}{5}$ $\qquad$ $\dfrac{3}{8}$

$\dfrac{4}{7}$ $\qquad$ $\dfrac{7}{10}$

$\dfrac{2}{7}$ $\qquad$ $\dfrac{3}{7}$

$\dfrac{4}{9}$ $\qquad$ $\dfrac{5}{7}$

C

$\dfrac{3}{10}$ $\qquad$ $\dfrac{5}{10}$

$\dfrac{5}{10}$ $\qquad$ $\dfrac{2}{10}$

$\dfrac{9}{10}$ $\qquad$ $\dfrac{7}{10}$

$\dfrac{8}{10}$ $\qquad$ $\dfrac{3}{10}$

$\dfrac{6}{10}$ $\qquad$ $\dfrac{1}{10}$

$\dfrac{7}{10}$ $\qquad$ $\dfrac{4}{10}$

My pencils have broken in half! Complete the pencils by matching the pieces which add up to 1.

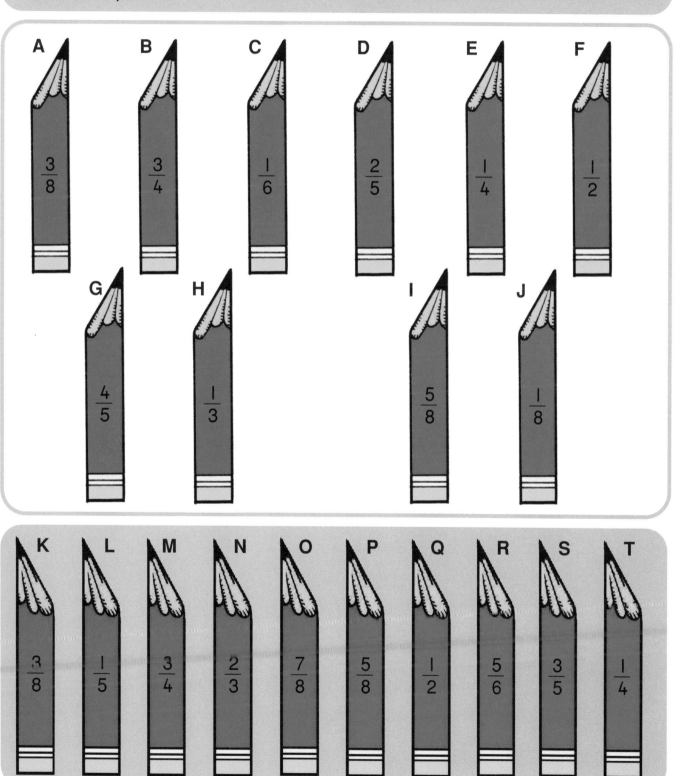

A $\frac{3}{8}$ B $\frac{3}{4}$ C $\frac{1}{6}$ D $\frac{2}{5}$ E $\frac{1}{4}$ F $\frac{1}{2}$

G $\frac{4}{5}$ H $\frac{1}{3}$ I $\frac{5}{8}$ J $\frac{1}{8}$

K $\frac{3}{8}$ L $\frac{1}{5}$ M $\frac{3}{4}$ N $\frac{2}{3}$ O $\frac{7}{8}$ P $\frac{5}{8}$ Q $\frac{1}{2}$ R $\frac{5}{6}$ S $\frac{3}{5}$ T $\frac{1}{4}$

Mel and Nigel earn the following amounts for helping Dad.
They share the money so that they each receive half.
How much money did each child get for each job?

Cleaning the car £6   Each received £_____

Walking the dog £2   Each received £_____

Cleaning the kitchen £8   Each received £_____

Cleaning the windows for a month £18   Each received £_____

After cleaning the windows, Dad brought out 18 biscuits.
Mel ate a third of them and Nigel ate half of them.

How many biscuits did Nigel eat?   _____

How many biscuits did Mel eat?   _____

How many biscuits were left?   _____

Mel and Nigel shared a bag of twenty
chocolates with Razia and Michael.

How many chocolates did each person get? _____

Four children divide this bar of chocolate between them.

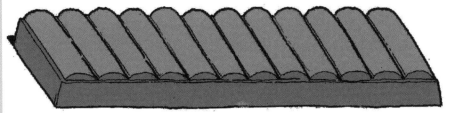

What fraction of the chocolate did each child get?   _____

How many pieces of chocolate did each child get?   _____

An identical bar of chocolate is divided between three children.

What fraction of the bar does each child receive?   _____

How many pieces of chocolate does each child have? _____

This packet of sweets is shared between 10 children.

What fraction of the sweets did each child receive? _____

How many sweets did each child get? _____

How did you work this out? _____

_____

_____

Look at each group of 3 cakes. For each group decide which shaded piece is the smallest, which is the largest and which comes in between. Write your answers next to the fractions.

A

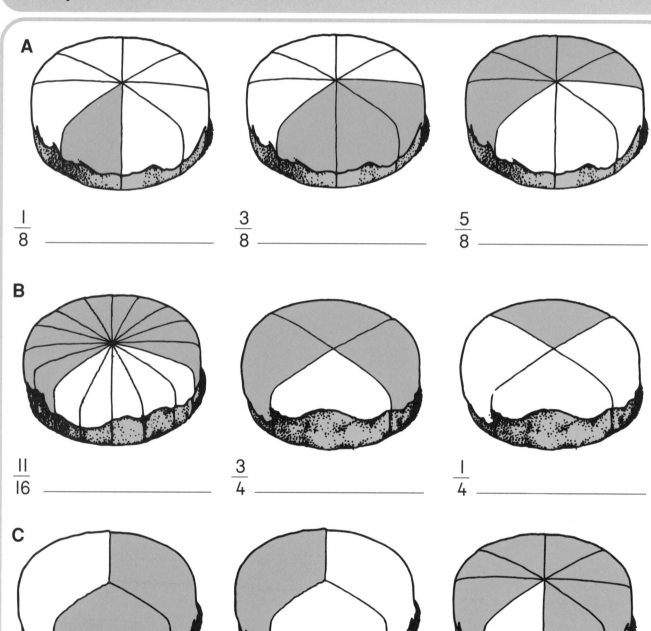

$\dfrac{1}{8}$ _____

$\dfrac{3}{8}$ _____

$\dfrac{5}{8}$ _____

B

$\dfrac{11}{16}$ _____

$\dfrac{3}{4}$ _____

$\dfrac{1}{4}$ _____

C

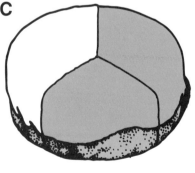

$\dfrac{2}{3}$ _____

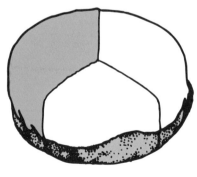

$\dfrac{1}{3}$ _____

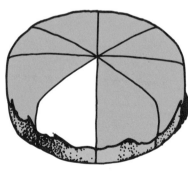

$\dfrac{7}{8}$ _____

If the fraction is bigger than $\frac{1}{2}$ put a tick in the box.
If the fraction is smaller than $\frac{1}{2}$ put a cross in the box.

A $\frac{1}{3}$ ☐

B $\frac{2}{3}$ ☐

C $\frac{5}{8}$ ☐

D $\frac{6}{7}$ ☐

E $\frac{3}{4}$ ☐

F $\frac{1}{4}$ ☐

G $\frac{7}{10}$ ☐

H $\frac{2}{6}$ ☐

I $\frac{3}{10}$ ☐

J $\frac{3}{10}$ ☐

K $\frac{3}{8}$ ☐

L $\frac{8}{12}$ ☐

M $\frac{4}{7}$ ☐

N $\frac{4}{5}$ ☐

O $\frac{5}{12}$ ☐

P $\frac{5}{8}$ ☐

Q $\frac{6}{8}$ ☐

R $\frac{1}{8}$ ☐

S $\frac{2}{9}$ ☐

T $\frac{3}{7}$ ☐

U $\frac{5}{6}$ ☐

V $\frac{3}{5}$ ☐

W $\frac{7}{8}$ ☐

X $\frac{11}{12}$ ☐

Top tip:

To help you, look at the **numerator** and decide whether it is bigger than half of the **denominator.** If it is, the fraction is bigger than a half.

Fill in the missing numbers and fractions in the sentences below.

This bar of chocolate has been shared

between _____ children.

They each get _____ of the chocolate.

This bar of chocolate has been shared

between _____ children.

They each get _____ of the chocolate.

This bar of chocolate has been shared

between _____ children.

They each get _____ of the chocolate.

This bar of chocolate has been shared

between _____ children.

They each get _____ of the chocolate.

Each bar of chocolate must be divided equally between some children.
The fraction of the chocolate that they all must receive is shown on the right.
Draw lines to correctly divide up the chocolate, and say how many pieces
each child gets.

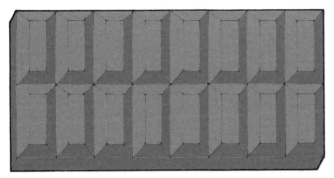

Divide the chocolate so that each child in a group gets $\frac{1}{4}$.

Each child gets _____ pieces.

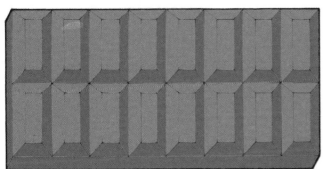

Divide this chocolate so that each child in a group gets $\frac{1}{8}$.

Each child gets _____ pieces.

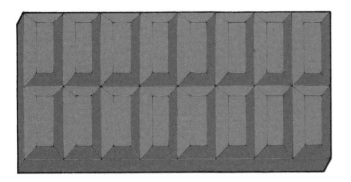

Divide this chocolate so that each child in a group gets $\frac{1}{2}$.

Each child gets _____ pieces.

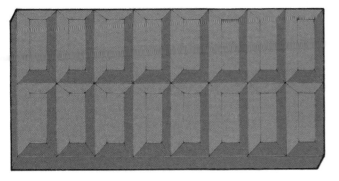

Divide this chocolate so that each child in a group gets $\frac{1}{16}$.

Each child gets _____ pieces.

Complete the sentences below each pattern
by filling in the missing numbers.

I in every 3 is coloured.

So _____ in every 6 are coloured,

and _____ in every 9 are coloured.

2 in every 3 are coloured.

So _____ in every 6 are coloured,

and _____ in every 9 are coloured.

5 in every 6 are coloured.

So _____ in every 12 are coloured,

and _____ in every 18 are coloured.

Complete the posters below by filling in the missing numbers.

A

Sweets:
10 sweets in every tube

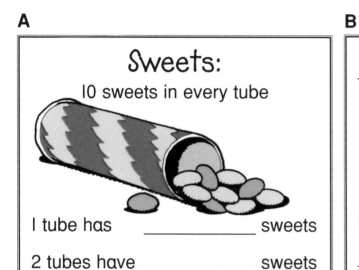

1 tube has	_____ sweets
2 tubes have	_____ sweets
3 tubes have	_____ sweets
4 tubes have	_____ sweets
5 tubes have	_____ sweets

B

Cookies:
5 cookies on every plate

1 plate has	_____ cookies
_____	plates have 10 cookies
3 plates have	_____ cookies
_____	plates have 20 cookies
5 plates have	_____ cookies

C

BUILD A JIGSAW:
for every 2 pieces collected you get 1 extra

2 pieces gives	_____ extra
4 pieces gives	_____ extra
6 pieces gives	_____ extra
8 pieces gives	_____ extra
10 pieces gives	_____ extra

D

Monsters!

SEND 4 TOKENS
FOR 1 MONSTER

4 tokens gets	_____ MONSTER!
_____	tokens gets 2 MONSTERS!
12 tokens gets	_____ MONSTERS!
16 tokens gets	_____ MONSTERS!
_____	tokens gets 5 MONSTERS!

What fraction of the larger shape is the smaller shape?

The first one has been done for you

A

$$\frac{2}{3}$$

B

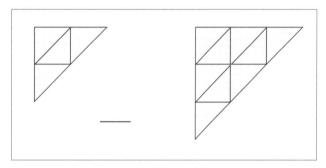

____

C

____

D

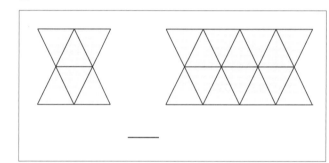

____

E

____

F

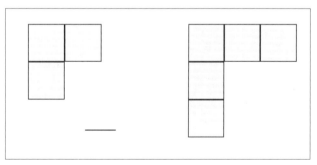

____

G

____

H

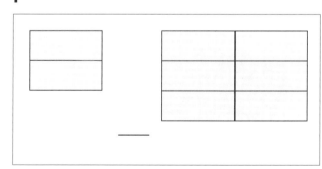

____

Add up the value of each group of coins in the box.
Then use this to find what fraction the smaller amount is
of the larger amount. The first one has been done for you.

A

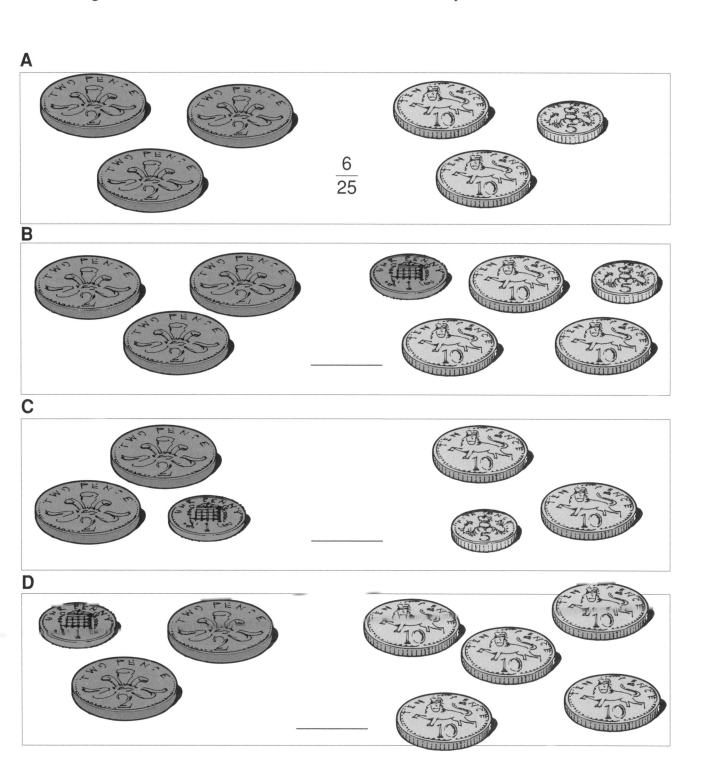

$\dfrac{6}{25}$

B

C

D

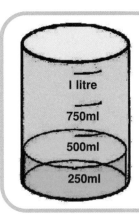

How much of this jar is full?   _____ml

What fraction of a litre is this?   _____

Look at these jars. What fraction of each jar is filled with liquid?
How many millilitres of liquid are there in each jar?
Each mark on the sides of the jars shows 100ml.

A   **B**   **C**

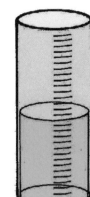

_____   _____   _____

_____   _____   _____

At a party there are 30 children. Each child has a cup that holds $\frac{1}{10}$ litre of juice.

How many litres of juice do you need to fill all the cups? _____

There are four litres of custard.
How many $\frac{1}{4}$-litre bowls can be filled?   _____

About what fraction of the children will get custard?   _____

Remember: I metre = 100 centimetres
        I kilometre = 1000 metres

Fill in each box with the correct answer.

A A car travels $\frac{1}{2}$ km. How many metres has it travelled so far?

B It travels another 750 metres. How many metres has it travelled so far?

C It travels another $\frac{3}{4}$ km. How many metres has it travelled now?

25cm is what fraction of I metre? _____

What is half I metre in centimetres? _____

Order the amounts of money from the smallest to the largest.

Label them 1 (smallest) to 5 (largest).

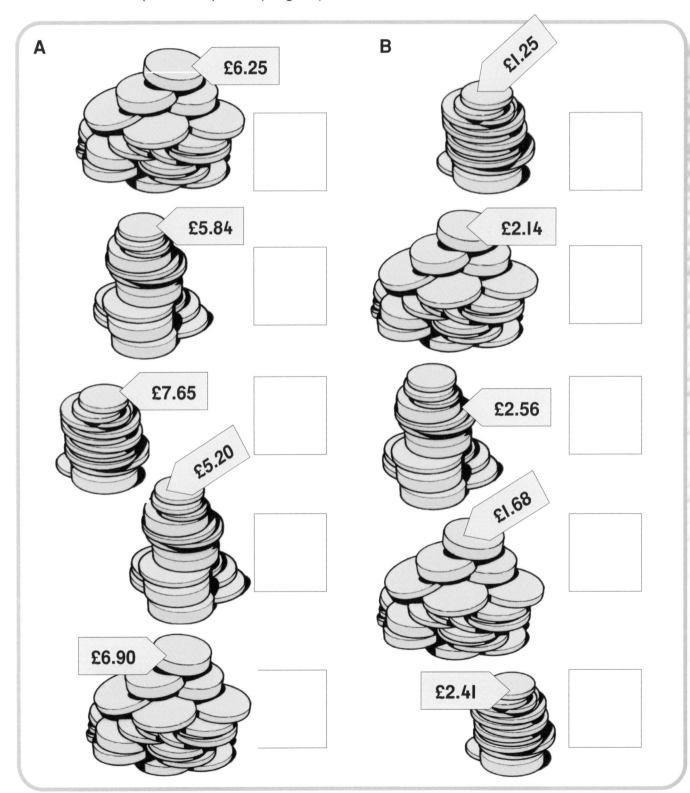

A

£6.25

£5.84

£7.65

£5.20

£6.90

B

£1.25

£2.14

£2.56

£1.68

£2.41

Who has saved the most money in their piggy bank?
Write the children's names in order, from the largest
amount saved to the least amount saved.

A

£3.64 ← James

Jenny → £2.98

£4.20 ← Mark

Mary → £3.25

£2.18 ← Robin

Rosie → £1.63

1 _____

2 _____

3 _____

4 _____

5 _____

6 _____

B

£2.99 ← Anne

Alan → £3.49

£2.15 ← Barbara

Ben → £4.25

£4.52 ← Carolyn

Colin → £2.36

1 _____

2 _____

3 _____

4 _____

5 _____

6 _____

How much of each pizza has been eaten?
Write the answer as a fraction and as a decimal.

A 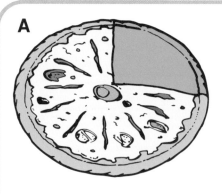 **B** 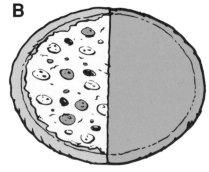 **C**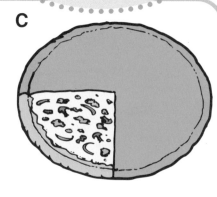

$\frac{1}{4}$ / 0.25 _____ / _____ _____ / _____

D 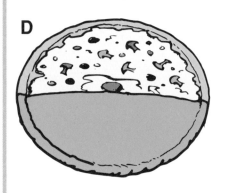 **E** 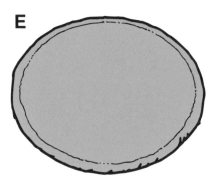 **F**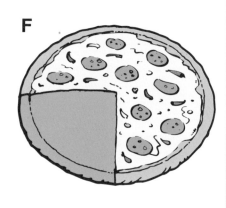

_____ / _____ _____ / _____ _____ / _____

G 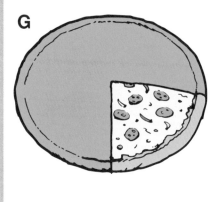 **H** 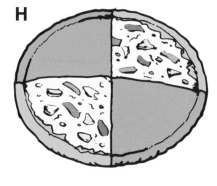 **I**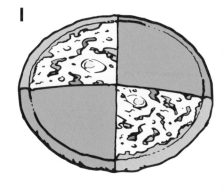

_____ / _____ _____ / _____ _____ / _____

Below each diagram write in the decimal and the fraction of the shaded area.

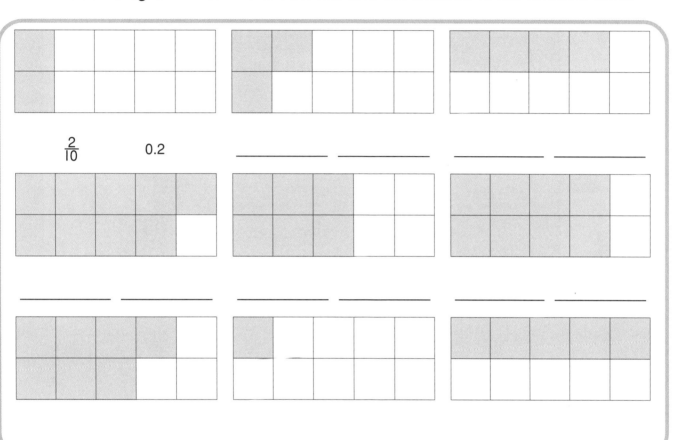

$\frac{2}{10}$ 0.2

_____ _____

_____ _____

_____ _____

_____ _____

_____ _____

_____ _____

_____ _____

Colour in the correct fraction of the diagrams below.

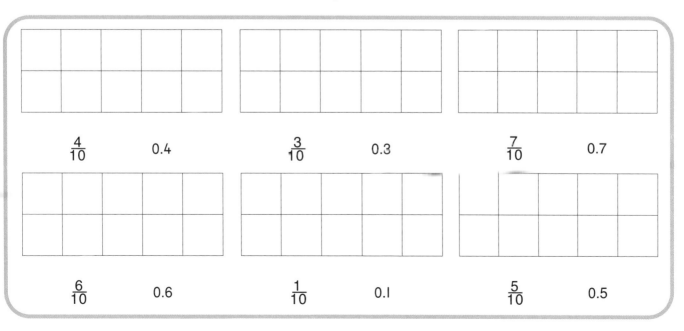

$\frac{4}{10}$ 0.4 $\frac{3}{10}$ 0.3 $\frac{7}{10}$ 0.7

$\frac{6}{10}$ 0.6 $\frac{1}{10}$ 0.1 $\frac{5}{10}$ 0.5

Show your workings here:

Michael left his maths book out and his dog walked all over it with muddy paws! Can you help Michael work out what numbers or signs have been hidden by the muddy pawmarks?

6 + 🐾 = 13 ____   12 + 🐾 = 18 ____

20 + 🐾 = 35 ____   35 + 🐾 = 60 ____

🐾 + 8 = 12 ____   🐾 + 15 = 20 ____

🐾 + 20 = 30 ____   🐾 + 45 = 100 ____

10 – 🐾 = 7 ____   16 – 🐾 = 9 ____

30 – 🐾 = 24 ____   60 – 🐾 = 35 ____

🐾 – 3 = 5 ____   🐾 – 8 = 12 ____

🐾 – 30 = 50 ____   🐾 – 25 = 75 ____

6 🐾 5 = 11 ____   14 🐾 8 = 22 ____

16 🐾 9 = 25 ____   35 🐾 15 = 50 ____

6 🐾 5 = 1 ____   14 🐾 8 = 6 ____

16 🐾 9 = 7 ____   35 🐾 15 = 20 ____

Answer these riddles. The answers are either one number
or a pair of numbers.

When you add us together we make 12.
The difference between us is 6. _____ _____

When you add us together we make 8.
When you multiply us together we make 15. _____ _____

I am bigger than 46 and smaller than 48. _____

I am twice as big as 12. _____

When you add me to myself I make 16. _____

When you add us together we make 24.
One of us is twice as big as the other. _____ _____

The difference between us is 5.
When you multiply us together we make 14. _____ _____

One of us is twice as big as the other.
The difference between us is 7. _____ _____

When you add me to any number, I do not change it. _____

When you multiply me by myself I make 25. _____

Show your workings here:

In a magic square the numbers in each row, each column and each diagonal add up to the same answer.

8	1	6
3	5	7
4	9	2

This is a magic square because the rows add up to 15:

8 + 1 + 6 = 15   3 + 5 + 7 = 15   4 + 9 + 2 = 15

the up and down columns add up to 15:

8 + 3 + 4 = 15   1 + 5 + 9 = 15   6 + 7 + 2 = 15

and so do the diagonals across the square:

8 + 5 + 2 = 15   4 + 5 + 6 = 15

Look at these squares. Put a tick by the ones which are magic and a cross by the ones which are not.

1
12	5	10
7	9	11
8	13	6

_____

2
3	5	9
4	8	2
7	1	6

_____

3
17	3	13
7	11	15
6	9	25

_____

4
7	12	5
8	9	7
10	3	11

_____

5
29	8	23
14	20	26
17	32	11

_____

6
13	15	12
21	11	3
6	9	25

_____

Can you work out the missing numbers in these magic squares?

16	2	12
6	10	
8		

12	5	
7	9	
8		

	7	17
	15	
13	23	

26	12	22
16	20	

10		6
	12	
18		14

3		
	6	
7		9

In this magic triangle each side adds up to 12.
Can you put in the missing numbers?

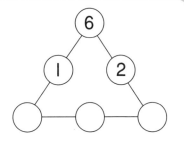

In this magic triangle each side adds up to 10.
Can you put in the missing numbers?

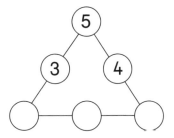

In this magic triangle each side adds up to 16.
Can you put in the missing numbers?

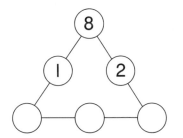

One way of solving a problem is called 'trial and error'.
You make a guess at the answer and then test it to see if it is right.
You can use this method to solve number puzzles.

Example:
We are two numbers that add up to 12 and multiply together to make 32.
What are we?

Think of some number pairs that add up to 12:

1 + 11   2 + 10   3 + 9   4 + 8   5 + 7   6 + 6

and then test them to see which multiply to make 32:

1 x 11 = 11   2 x 10 = 20   3 x 9 = 27   4 x 8 = 32

so the answer is 4 and 8.

You don't need to write all this out. You can do it in your head or make rough jottings.

Try to find the number pairs that answer these riddles:
We add up to 13 and multiply together to make 40.

_____ and _____

We add up to 12 and multiply together to make 35.

_____ and _____

We add up to 11 and multiply together to make 18.

_____ and _____

We add up to 14 and multiply together to make 48.

_____ and _____

Consecutive numbers are numbers that come next
to each other, such as:
3, 4, 5, or 8, 9, 10, or 32, 33, 34.
You could use trial and error on these problems –
but there might be a quicker way!

Example:
Find three consecutive numbers that add up to 33.

33 is near 30.
You know that 10 + 10 + 10 = 30, so the numbers must be near 10.

Try 9, 10 and 11.
They add up to only 30 so the numbers need to be a bit bigger.

Try 10, 11 and 12.
10 + 11 + 12 = 33, so you've found the answer!

Find three consecutive numbers that add up to 21.

_____ _____ _____

Find three consecutive numbers that add up to 48.

_____ _____ _____

Find three consecutive **odd** numbers that add up to 27.

_____ _____ _____

Find three consecutive **even** numbers that add up to 54.

_____ _____ _____

Can you find a quicker way to do these?

Some puzzles involve working out missing numbers. If only one number is missing there is usually only one answer.

$17 + ? = 20$ The answer must be 3.
$30 - ? = 16$ The answer must be 14.

See if you can work out the missing numbers in these puzzles.

$25 + \_\_\_ = 34$ $35 - \_\_\_ = 21$

$\_\_\_ + 16 = 29$ $\_\_\_ - 12 = 24$

If there are several numbers missing there could be more than one right answer.

Choose three numbers from 1, 2, 3, 4 and 5 to fill in the blanks.

$\_\_\_\_ \_\_\_\_ + \_\_\_\_ = 17$ The answer could be
$13 + 4 = 17$
or $14 + 3 = 17$
or $15 + 2 = 17$
or $12 + 5 = 17$

See if you can find the missing numbers which will make these calculations right. Sometimes there is more than one answer.
Use 1, 2, 3, 4 and 5.

$\_\_\_\_ \_\_\_\_ + \_\_\_\_ = 36$ $\_\_\_\_ \_\_\_\_ - \_\_\_\_ = 38$

$3\_\_\_\_ + \_\_\_\_7 = 52$ $4\_\_\_\_ - \_\_\_\_6 = 19$

Can you split the set of numbers 1, 2, 3, 4, 5, 6, 7 and 8 into two sets of four, so that each set totals 18?

One way would be: 1, 2, 7, 8 and 3, 4, 5, 6

Can you find any other ways of doing it?

_____, _____, _____, _____ and _____, _____, _____, _____.

_____, _____, _____, _____ and _____, _____, _____, _____.

Can you split the set of numbers 1, 2, 3, 4, 5, 6, 7, 8 and 9 into three sets of three, so that each set totals 15?

_____, _____, _____ and _____, _____, _____ and _____, _____, _____.

Can you find another way of doing it?

_____, _____, _____ and _____, _____, _____ and _____, _____, _____.

Each shape can be cut into two identical halves with a single straight line. Draw where the lines should go.

The first one is done for you.

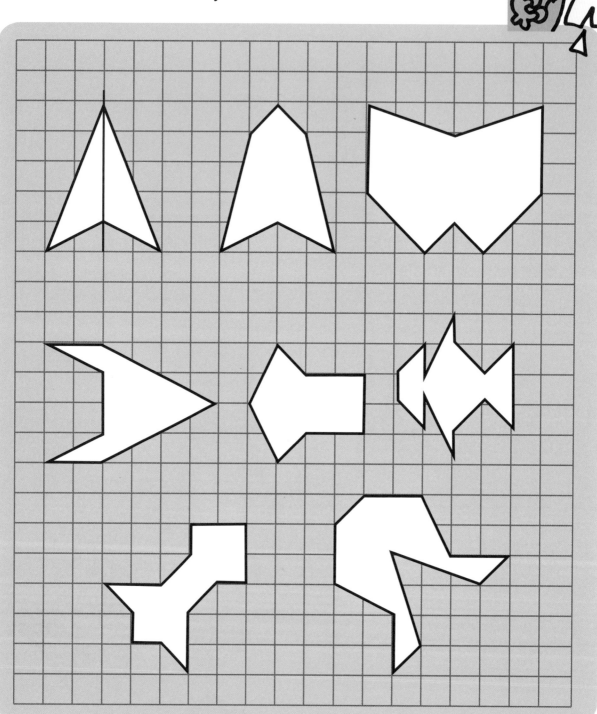

Shape Symmetry

Can you draw in the missing bits to make these shapes symmetrical?

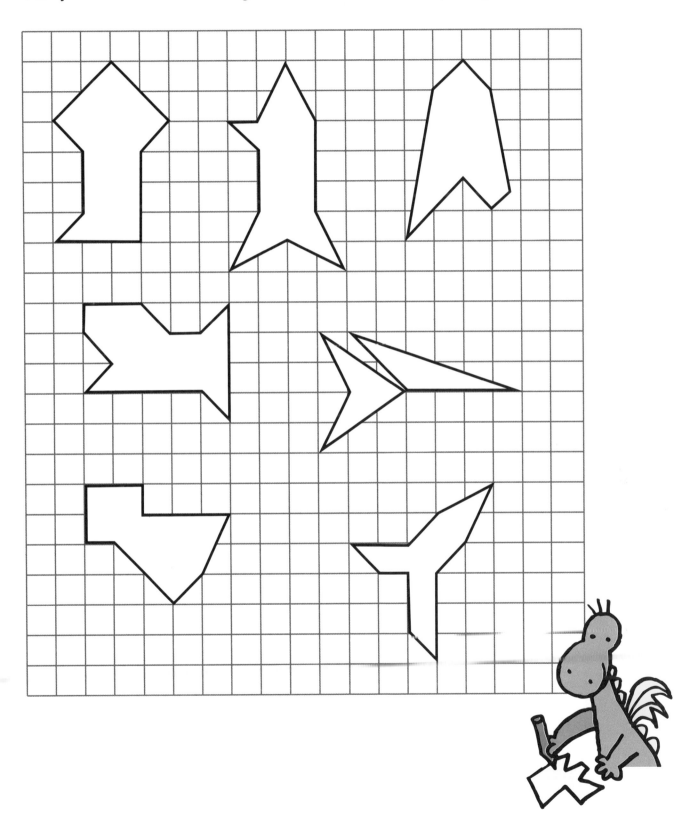

 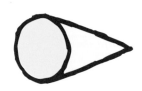 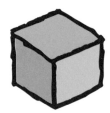 

How many triangles can you see in this shape?

_____

Jodie picked a solid shape out of the shape box at school.
She drew round each face of the shape.

What was the shape she picked? _____

Chris picked a different shape and drew round the faces.

What shape did he pick? _____

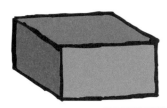   

Julie, James, Scott and Jessica had to describe the 3D shape they picked out of the box.

Can you identify the shapes from their descriptions?

Julie says, 'All of its faces are squares.'

_____

James says, 'Two of its faces are circles.'

_____

Scott says, 'Its faces are three pairs of rectangles.'

_____

Julie says, 'It has one flat face and one curved face.'

_____

Michael picked a triangular prism.
How would he describe it?

_____

_____

The children are making
a school magazine.

There are 32 children in the class.
They are working in pairs to write
articles for the magazine.
How many articles will be written?

_____

The magazine has 8 pages.
How many articles will there be
on each page?

_____

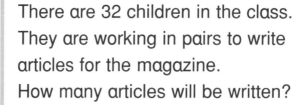

They need 4 sheets of paper for
each magazine. They decide to print
60 copies of the magazine.
How much paper will they need?

_____

The school copier prints 40 sheets
of paper a minute.
How long will it take to print the magazines?

_____

They decide to sell the magazine at the school fête for 50p a copy. How much money will they make if they sell them all?

_____

They only sell 35 copies. How many copies are left unsold?

_____

How much money do they make by selling 35 copies at 50p each?

_____

They need £8 of the money to pay for printing the magazine. They give the rest to a charity. How much is there to give to charity?

_____

Show your workings here:

Jodie, Michael, Natasha and Joe collect their sponsor money for the 50 lengths they have swum.

Jodie's grannny gives her 10p for each length she swam.

How much does she give Jodie? _____

Michael's uncle gives him 5p for each length.

How much does he give him? _____

Natasha's friend gives her 2p for each length.

How much does she give her? _____

Joe's dad gives him £5 altogether.

How much is this for each length? _____

Show your workings here:

How much did these people give them altogether?

Jodie's granny	£
Michael's uncle	£
Natasha's friend	£
Joe's dad	£ 5.00
Total	£

The four children finish collecting their sponsor money.
They sort the money out. Help them work out how much
money they have collected:

5 £2 coins = £_____   20 £l coins = £_____

l0 50p coins = £_____   l0 20p coins = £_____

20 l0p coins = £_____   20 5p coins = £_____

50 2p coins = £_____   100 lp coins = £_____

Altogether they have: £_____

They take the money to the bank to change into larger notes and coins.

They change the   5   £2 coins for _____ £5 notes.

They change the 20   £l coins for _____£l0 notes.

They change the l0 50p coins for _____ £5 note.

They change the l0 20p coins for _____ £l coins.

They change the 20 l0p coins for _____ £l coins.

They change the 20   5p coins for _____ £l coin.

They change the 50   2p coins for _____ £l coin.

They change the 100   lp coins for _____ £l coin.

It's Sally's birthday soon. Her mum says that Sally can organise her party herself.

Sally invites 6 children to her party.
She makes up party bags of sweets for everyone.
The sweets in each bag cost 80p.
How much will all the bags cost?

_____

She needs some music for the party.
She buys a CD for £12.50 and a cassette tape for £5.25.
How much did she spend?

_____

She pays for the CD and tape with a £20 note.
How much change does she get?

_____

She looks in the supermarket for drinks.
She could buy four 1 litre bottles of orange at £1.50 each,
or two 2 litre bottles for £2.75 each.
Which would be cheaper and by how much?

_____

Sally decides to make up a fruit punch for the party.
Work out the total cost of the punch.

I bottle of orange juice at £1.50	£
4 apples at 30p each	£
2 bottles of lemonade at £1.25 each	£
3 oranges at 25p each	£
2 lemons at 45p each	£
Total	£

How much change will she get from a £10 note?

_____

Show your workings here:

The children help out at the shop.

Jodie's job is to weigh out the potatoes.
She puts the potatoes in bags.
Each bag can hold 5kg of potatoes.
How many bags will she need for 100kg of potatoes? _____

Michael is helping with the apples.
Each apple weighs about 150g.
He has to put them in bags which hold 1kg.
Roughly how many apples will he put in each bag? _____

Natasha is tying up the bags with string.
She needs 50cm of string for each bag.
How many bags can she tie up with 10m of string? _____

Joe has the job of putting orange juice into bottles.
Each bottle holds $\frac{1}{2}$ litre.
How many bottles will he need for 20 litres of juice? _____

Show your workings here:

The shopkeeper asks them to put out labels for the items on the shelves. Can you work out which label goes with which item?

Draw lines from the items to the correct labels.

Show your workings here:

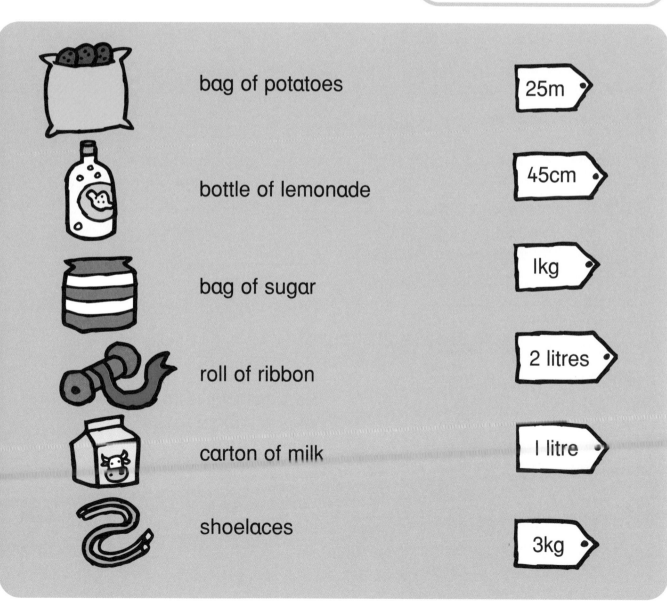

bag of potatoes

bottle of lemonade

bag of sugar

roll of ribbon

carton of milk

shoelaces

25m

45cm

1kg

2 litres

1 litre

3kg

Here is another page from a calendar.

January

Sunday	Monday	Tuesday	Wednesday	Thursday	Friday	Saturday
		1	2	3	4	5
6	7	8	9	10	11	12
13	14	15	16	17	18	19
20	21	22	23	24	25	26
27	28	29	30	31		

On which day does the month start?

_____

On which day does the month finish?

_____

How many days are there in the month?

_____

What day of the week is 17 January?

_____

Jessica goes on a two-week holiday on 10 January. On what day does she come back?

_____

Which day is 4 days after Monday?

_____

Tim's birthday is on 1 February. What day will this be?

_____

The children at Hayland School are putting on a special evening.

They make up a programme for the different events.

Programme

7.30 pm   Choir

7.45 pm   Gym Display

8.05 pm   Recorder Group

8.15 pm   School Band

8.25 pm   Interval

8.45 pm   Play

Which item started at a quarter to eight?

_____

Which item started at a quarter past eight?

_____

What was on at 8.00 pm?

_____

How long did the interval last?

_____

The play lasted for half an hour. At what time did the evening finish?

_____

Ben and Kevin are planning what TV programmes they will watch this evening, using this TV Guide.

TV Guide

DDCI		DDC2		ITB	
5.30	People Next Door	5.30	Near and Far	5.30	Weather Report
6.00	News	6.00	The Sampsons	5.40	Local News
6.15	Watchcat	6.30	Pulsebeat	6.15	THI Thursday
6.40	Top of the Flops	7.15	Changing Houses	7.00	Summerdale
7.30	Showtime	7.40	One Man and his Pig	7.30	Queen Street
8.15	Star Trip	8.10	Jasper Cabbage	8.00	Gardener's Life
10.05	Late News	8.45	Athletics	8.25	Badgerside
		9.40	News-square	9.15	North Park

What time does The Sampsons start?

_____

How long does Pulsebeat last?

_____

How long does Top of the Flops last?

_____

How long does the film Star Trip last?

_____

Which programme starts on DDC2 at 7.40?

_____

What will be showing on ITB at 7.45?

_____

At the end of Badgerside they turn to DDCI.
What programme is on?

_____

How much have they missed of it?

_____

On Saturday a group of children from Tinyville decide to go shopping in Bigtown. They look at the bus timetable to plan their journey.

Bus Timetable

Tinyville to Bigtown				Bigtown to Tinyville			
Tinyville	8.15 am	9.10 am	10.22 am	Bigtown	1.00 pm	2.15 pm	3.32 pm
Midton	8.30 am	9.25 am	10.37 am	Fargate	1.20 pm	2.35 pm	3.52 pm
Fargate	8.40 am	9.35 am	10.47 am	Midton	1.30 pm	2.45 pm	4.02 pm
Bigtown	9.00 am	9.55 am	11.07 am	Tinyville	1.45 pm	3.00 pm	4.17 pm

What is the earliest bus they can catch from Tinyville?

_____

What time would it get to Bigtown?

_____

How long does the journey take from Tinyville to Bigtown?

_____

How long is the journey from Midton to Fargate?

_____

They want to be in Bigtown by 10.00 am. What time must they get the bus from Tinyville?

_____

They arrive in Bigtown at 9.55 am. How long would they have in town if they caught the first bus back?

_____

Their parents say they must be home by 3.30 pm. What time must they get the bus in Bigtown?

_____

They catch this bus but it is held up for 12 minutes by roadworks at Midton. Will they get home in time?

_____

The children are going to hold a bring and buy sale at the school.

Joe brought a tray of cakes.
On the tray were 6 rows of 5 cakes.
How many cakes did he bring?

_____

Tina brought 4 plates.
On each plate were 7 scones.
How many scones did she bring?

_____

Jack brought 5 plates with 5 scones on each.
Did he bring more or less than Tina?

_____

How many more or less?

_____

The tables and chairs are set out in the hall.

There are:
5 tables with 4 chairs each
5 tables with 8 chairs each
5 tables with 9 chairs each

Were there enough chairs to seat 100 people?

_____

Mary sold 24 cakes at 10p each.
How much money did she make?

_____

Jane sold 15 buns at 20p each.
How much money did she make?

_____

Mike brought sandwiches.
He brought 15 beef sandwiches, 23 ham sandwiches
and 25 cheese sandwiches.
How many sandwiches did he bring altogether?

_____

Carla bought some cakes from the cake stall.

Scones were 16p each.
Apple tarts were 15p each.
Chocolate muffins were 14p each.

She bought 6 of one kind of cake.
She spent £1 and got 10p change.
Which kind of cake did she buy?

_____

Tom and Emma are doing a survey of what games children like to play in the playground.
There are 240 children in the school.

Half the children are boys and half are girls.
How many boys are there?

_____

A quarter of the boys like to play football.
How many boys like to play football?

_____

A third of the girls like to play football.
How many girls is this?

_____

Half the children play on the field.
A quarter of the children prefer the playground.
The rest like to sit in the quiet area.
What fraction sit in the quiet area?

_____

20 children are skipping.
5 of them are using blue ropes.
What fraction is this?

_____

Tom and Emma ask a group of 12
children what their favourite item of
playground equipment is.
6 say the climbing frame.
4 say the scramble net.
2 say the sandpit.

What fraction preferred the
climbing frame?

_____

What fraction preferred the
scramble net?

_____

Tom and Emma asked 16 children if
they would like playtime to be longer.
Three-quarters of them said
they would.
How many children was this?

_____

One-fifth of the children eat crisps at
playtime.
Two-fifths eat biscuits.
The rest eat fruit.
What fraction eat fruit?

_____

Fill in the answers on this addition square.

+	1	2	3	4	5	6	7	8	9	10
1	2									
2		4	5	6	7	8	9	10	11	12
3			6	7	8	9	10	11	12	13
4				8	9	10	11	12	13	14
5	6				10	11				
6	7					12	13			
7	8						14	15		
8	9							16	17	
9	10								18	19
10	11	12	13	14	15	16	17	18	19	20

We call the number of times something happens "frequency".

How frequently does each group of answers appear?

Answer	Frequency
1–4	
5–8	
9–12	
13–16	
17–20	

Which answers have the highest frequency? _____

Why do you think these answers appear the most? _____

Which answers have the lowest frequency? _____

Why do you think these answers appear least? _____

Which number does not appear at all in the answers? _____

Why does this number not appear at all? _____

This block graph shows the number of television sets sold at a shop in one week.

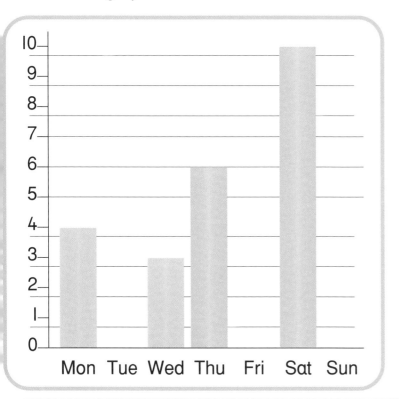

On Tuesday they sold half as many televisions as on Thursday.
Fill in the number of televisions sold on Tuesday.

On Friday they sold twice as many televisions as on Wednesday.
Fill in the graph to show how many televisions they sold on Friday.

On which day did they sell the most televisions? _____

What was the highest number of televisions sold? _____

On which day do you think the shop was closed? _____

Explain your answer. _____

_____

The shop began the week with 50 televisions.
How many televisions do they still have left? _____

We use **tally marks** to count things.

1 = I		6 = ⱧⱮ I
2 = II		7 = ⱧⱮ II
3 = III		8 = ⱧⱮ III
4 = IIII		9 = ⱧⱮ IIII
5 = ⱧⱮ		10 = ⱧⱮ ⱧⱮ and so on.

Count the tally marks and write how many there are.

ⱧⱮ ⱧⱮ II   = _____

ⱧⱮ I   = _____

ⱧⱮ ⱧⱮ ⱧⱮ ⱧⱮ ⱧⱮ   = _____

ⱧⱮ ⱧⱮ ⱧⱮ II   = _____

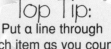

Count the vehicles in the traffic jam.

Lorry   _____

Car   _____

Motorbike   _____

TOTAL   _____

Use tally marks to count each group of items.

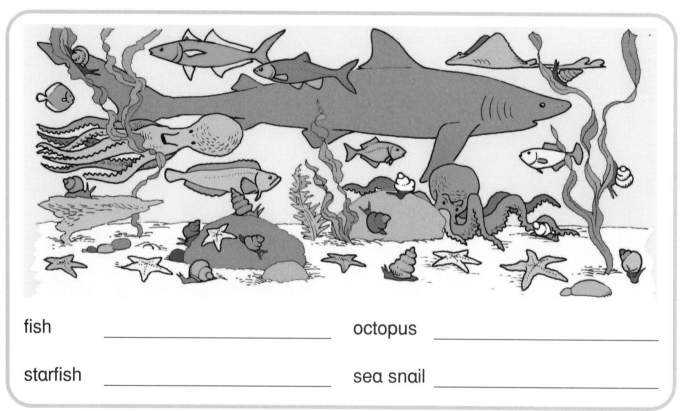

fish _____   octopus _____

starfish _____   sea snail _____

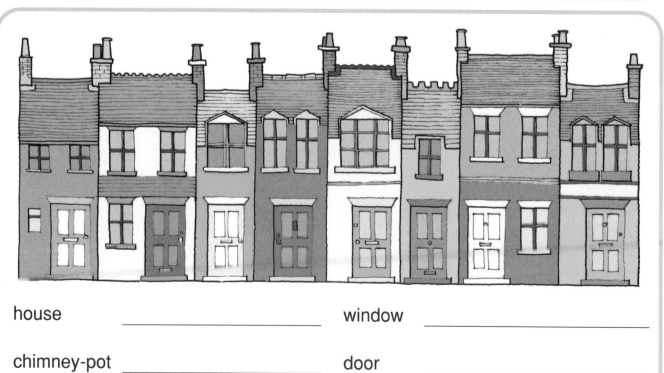

house _____   window _____

chimney-pot _____   door _____

This is a bar chart for the number of hours a family spent watching television over a two-week holiday.

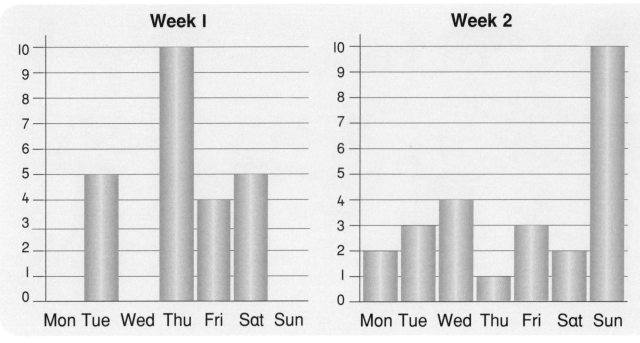

Complete the bar chart using this information.

The family watched twice as much television on the first Monday than on the second. The family watched half as much television on the first Wednesday than on the second.

Look at the bar chart and then answer these questions.

Two days of the holidays had very bad weather. On which days do you think the weather was worst?
Explain why you think this.

_____

_____

_____

_____

What day during the holiday do you think the family went out all day?
Explain why you think this.

_____

_____

_____

Which week did the family spend the most amount of time watching television? _____

Use the information in this chart to complete the bar chart.

Time	Cars Washed
8:00–9:00	9
9:00–10:00	4
10:00–11:00	3
11:00–12:00	8
12:00–1:00	6
1:00–2:00	3
2:00–3:00	2
3:00–4:00	3
4:00–5:00	1
5:00–6:00	10

Top Tip:
The title of a chart tells what it is about. Each axis measures something. On this one the side axis measures how many cars; the bottom axis measures time.

Give your chart a title. Name each axis.

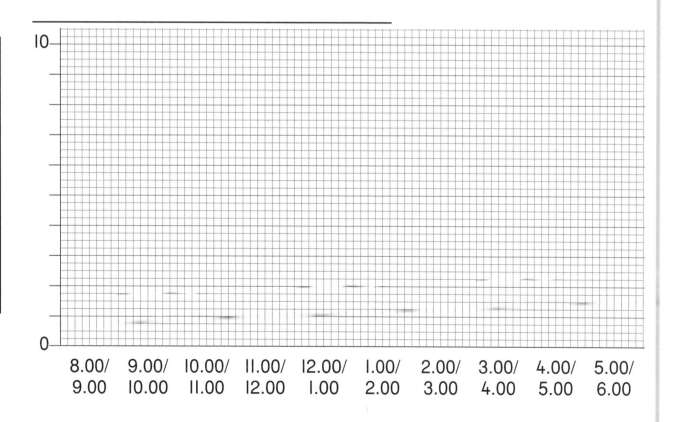

Use this information to complete the bar chart.

Time	Buses
8:00–9:00	10
9:00–10:00	5
10:00–11:00	3
11:00–12:00	2
12:00–1:00	6
1:00–2:00	4
2:00–3:00	3
3:00–4:00	2
4:00–5:00	3
5:00–6:00	10

Give your chart a title. Name each axis.

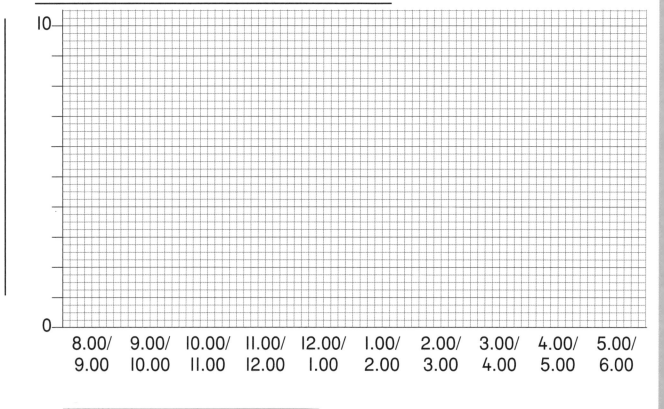

When does the greatest number of buses travel? _____

Why do you think there are more buses at these times? _____

A pictogram is a way of showing information.
It uses pictures to represent things.
This picture ⚊ means I person.

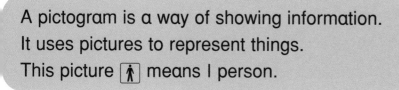

How many people do you think this picture shows? _____

Look at this pictogram. Write down next to the pictogram the number of people who go swimming each day.

Days	Swimming	How many?
Mon	⚊ ⚊ ⚊ ⚊ ⚊ ⚊ ⚊ ⚊	
Tue	⚊ ⚊ ⚊ ⚊ ⚊ ⚊ ⚊ ⚊ ⚊ ⚊ ⚊ ⚊	
Wed	⚊ ⚊ ⚊ ⚊ ⚊ ⚊ ⚊	
Thu	⚊ ⚊ ⚊ ⚊ ⚊ ⚊	
Fri	⚊ ⚊ ⚊ ⚊ ⚊	
Sat	⚊ ⚊ ⚊ ⚊ ⚊ ⚊ ⚊ ⚊	
Sun	⚊ ⚊ ⚊ ⚊ ⚊ ⚊ ⚊ ⚊ ⚊ ⚊	

What day did the greatest number of children go swimming? _____

What day did half that number go swimming? _____

What day did the least number of children go swimming? _____

Sometimes a pictogram is used to stand for
a number of people, things or events.

This cake stands for 10 cakes.

How many cakes does each of these pictograms stand for?

_____

_____

_____

Top Tip:

Half a car = 5 cars sold.

This car means that 10 cars have been sold.
How many cars did this company sell each month?

Month	Sales	How many?
Jan	🚗 🚗 🚗	
Feb	🚗 🚗	
Mar	🚗 🚗 🚗 🚗 🚗 🚗 🚗	
Apr	🚗	
May	🚗 🚗	
Jun	🚗	
Jul	🚗 🚗 🚗 🚗	
Aug	🚗 🚗 🚗 🚗 🚗 🚗	
Sep	🚗 🚗 🚗 🚗 🚗	
Oct	🚗 🚗	
Nov	🚗	
Dec	🚗 🚗 🚗	

This pictogram stands for the number of hot school meals eaten in a year.

$\boxed{\text{Y1}}$ = 20 plates

Here is a list of all the meals eaten each month.

Use the symbol above to show the information as a pictogram.

	Meals Eaten	Pictogram
January	ЖЖ ЖЖ ЖЖ ЖЖ ЖЖ ЖЖ ЖЖ ЖЖ ЖЖ	
February	ЖЖ ЖЖ ЖЖ ЖЖ ЖЖ ЖЖ ЖЖ	
March	ЖЖ ЖЖ ЖЖ ЖЖ ЖЖ ЖЖ	
April	ЖЖ ЖЖ ЖЖ ЖЖ ЖЖ	
May	ЖЖ ЖЖ ЖЖ ЖЖ	
June	ЖЖ ЖЖ ЖЖ ЖЖ	
July	ЖЖ ЖЖ	
August		
September	ЖЖ ЖЖ ЖЖ ЖЖ ЖЖ ЖЖ ЖЖ ЖЖ	
October	ЖЖ ЖЖ ЖЖ ЖЖ ЖЖ ЖЖ ЖЖ ЖЖ ЖЖ ЖЖ	
November	ЖЖ ЖЖ ЖЖ ЖЖ ЖЖ ЖЖ ЖЖ ЖЖ ЖЖ ЖЖ ЖЖ	
December	ЖЖ ЖЖ ЖЖ ЖЖ ЖЖ ЖЖ ЖЖ ЖЖ ЖЖ ЖЖ ЖЖ ЖЖ ЖЖ	

Why does the number go up during December? _____

What month do you think school is closed? _____

Explain your answer. _____

Which way of showing the information is easiest to understand? _____

Explain your answer. _____

When we have a large number of items to count,
we can use a pictogram to represent more than 1 of each item.

This pictogram represents 20 ferry crossings.

How many pictograms represent:

60 ferry crossings	_____	140 ferry crossings	_____
100 ferry crossings	_____	160 ferry crossings	_____
120 ferry crossings	_____	180 ferry crossings	_____

We can use part of a pictogram to represent a number, too:

This pictogram represents 20 ferry crossings.

This pictogram represents 15 ferry crossings – it is $\frac{3}{4}$ of the size so it represents $\frac{3}{4}$ of the number.

This pictogram represents 10 ferry crossings – it is half the size so it represents half the number.

This pictogram represents 5 ferry crossings – it is $\frac{1}{4}$ of the size so it represents $\frac{1}{4}$ of the number.

How many pictograms represent:

15 ferry crossings	_____	40 ferry crossings	_____
25 ferry crossings	_____	110 ferry crossings	_____

Write how many ferry crossings there are each month in the last column of the table. Then read the frequency table to answer the questions below.

Month	Number of ferry crossings	
January		
February		
March		
April		
May		
June		
July		
August		
September		
October		
November		
December		

Which month was quietest? _____

Which month was busiest? _____

Which month has half as many crossings as August? _____

Which two months had the same number of crossings? _____

Bar graph scales

Use this frequency chart to draw a bar chart.

What is the best increase for each interval?

_____

Remember that the interval is how much the numbers along the side go up by.

Theme park visitors for this year	
Month	**Thousand of visitors**
January	5
February	10
March	20
April	35
May	45
June	60
July	60
August	60
September	50
October	45
November	10
December	5

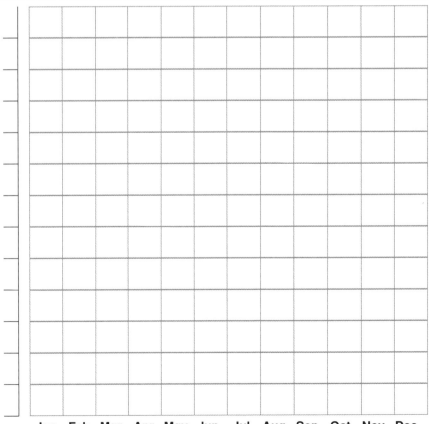

Jan Feb Mar Apr May Jun Jul Aug Sep Oct Nov Dec

Look at the computer sales carefully and the graph template shown below. Decide on the best interval to show all the information. It may help if you think of the numbers as being just below or just above the nearest multiple of 5. (For example, 23 is nearly 25.)

Look at the information below. It shows the number of computers sold during a year.

	Hundreds
Jan	33
Feb	29
Mar	22
Apr	17
May	12
Jun	14
Jul	19
Aug	23
Sep	24
Oct	28
Nov	30
Dec	39

Jan Feb Mar Apr May Jun Jul Aug Sep Oct Nov Dec

Why do you think they sold more computers during December and January?

_____

_____

_____

_____

Look at the information shown in this graph.

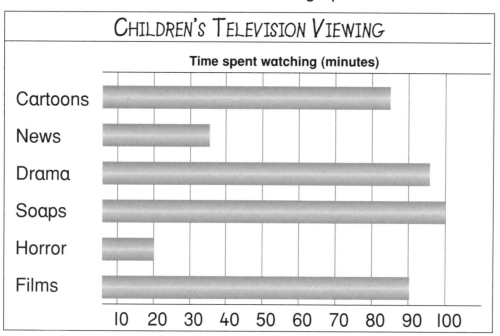

What did children spend most of their time watching?

_____

How many programmes were watched for longer than an hour?

_____

What is the least watched type of programme type?

_____

Which type of programme is watched for $1\frac{1}{2}$ hours?

_____

Which type of programme is watched for I hour longer than the news?

_____

If you wanted to put an advert on during a programme, which programme
would you choose? Explain your answer.

_____

Look at cooking times shown on this chart.

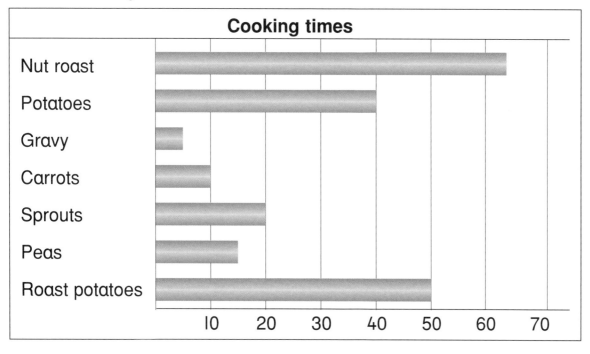

Which food takes the longest to prepare? _____

Imagine you had to prepare this meal for your family.

If the meal had to be ready at 1:00 in the afternoon what times would you have to start cooking each piece of food to make sure they were all ready at 1 o'clock?

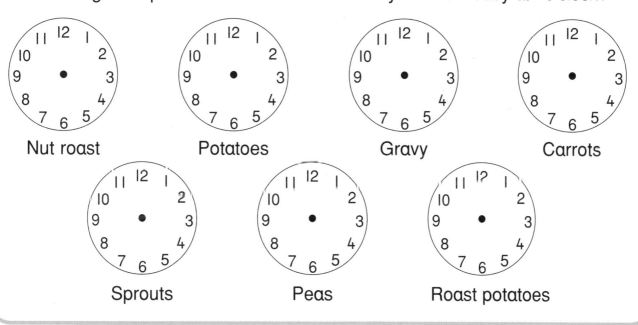

I conducted a survey among my friends.

I wanted to find out what they like to do at the weekend.

Collecting data and recording it in a frequency table

I gave them a list of activities. Then I ticked off the activities they liked.

	Computer games	Shopping	Swimming	Watching TV
Jenny	✔	✔	✔	
Mel		✔	✔	
Martin	✔	✔		
Jerry	✔		✔	
Charlie	✔		✔	✔
Vicci				

Use this frequency table to find out what your friends like to do.

Name	Computer games	Shopping	Swimming	Watching TV

A survey

Presenting the data

I drew a bar chart to show the results of the survey.

What my friends like to do at the weekend

Which two activities are the most popular?_____

Which activity was the least popular?_____

Now draw a bar chart for **your** survey.

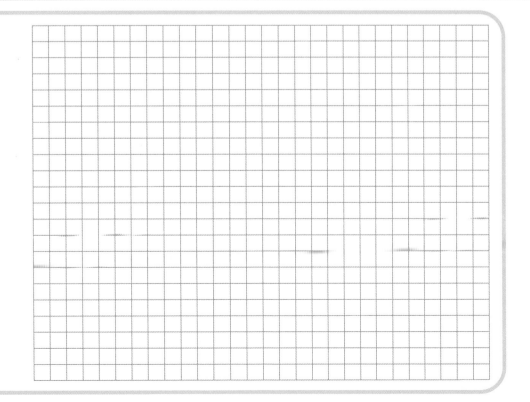

page 4
78 + 5 = 83, 124 + 8 = 132, 235 + 7 = 242, 337 + 4 = 341.
85 + 30 = 115, 124 + 40 = 164, 68 + 50 = 118, 95 + 20 = 115

page 5
0, 5, 10, 15, 20, 25, 30, 35, 40, 45.
8, 13, 18, 23, 28, 33, 38, 43, 48, 53.
6, 11, 16, 21, 26, 31, 36, 41, 46, 51.
9, 14, 19, 24, 29, 34, 39, 44, 49, 54.
7, 12, 17, 22, 27, 32, 37, 42, 47, 52.
3 + 5 + 7 + 5 + 2 = (3 + 7) + (5 + 5) + 2 = 10 + 10 + 2 = 20 + 2 = 22.
6 + 3 + 4 + 1 + 7 = (6 + 4) + (3 + 7) + 1 = 10 + 10 + 1 = 20 + 1 = 21.

page 6
56 + 9 = 65, 74 + 19 = 93, 87 + 29 = 116, 63 + 39 =102, 134 + 9 = 143,
236 + 19 = 255, 323 + 29 = 352, 354 + 39 = 393.
85 + 11 = 96, 64 + 21 = 85, 58 + 31 = 89, 72 + 41 = 113, 134 + 11 = 145,
435 + 21 = 456, 546 + 31 = 577, 227 + 41 = 268.
76 − 9 = 67, 86 − 19 = 67, 154 − 29 = 125, 345 − 39 = 306,
86 − 11 = 75, 93 − 21 = 72, 386 − 31 = 355, 556 − 41 = 515.

page 7
17 + 35 → 17 + 85 = 52, 62, 72, 82, 92, 102.
87 − 34 → 87 − 84 = 53, 43, 33, 23, 13, 3.
500 + 300 = 800, 5000 + 3000 = 8000, 700 − 200 = 500,
7000 − 2000 = 5000.

+	1	2	3	4	5	6	7	8	9	10
1	2	3	4	5	6	7	8	9	10	11
2	3	4	5	6	7	8	9	10	11	12
3	4	5	6	7	8	9	10	11	12	13
4	5	6	7	8	9	10	11	12	13	14
5	6	7	8	9	10	11	12	13	14	15
6	7	8	9	10	11	12	13	14	15	16
7	8	9	10	11	12	13	14	15	16	17
8	9	10	11	12	13	14	15	16	17	18
9	10	11	12	13	14	15	16	17	18	19
10	11	12	13	14	15	16	17	18	19	20

page 8
20 ÷ 2 = 10, 16 ÷ 2 = 8, 40 ÷ 5 = 8, 25 ÷ 5 = 5, 40 ÷ 10 = 4,
60 ÷ 10 = 6.
9, 7, 7, 3, 5, 8

page 9
Half: 12 = 6, 8 = 4, 20 = 10.
Double: 6 = 12, 4 = 8, 10 = 20.
14 x 2 → 20 x 2: 28, 30, 32, 34, 36, 38, 40.
Half 28 → 40: 14, 15, 16, 17, 18, 19, 20.

page 10
14 + 16 = 30, 18 + 22 = 40, 35 + 25 = 60, 37 + 23 = 60, 49 + 21 = 70,
48 + 22 = 70, 38 + 32 = 70, 57 + 33 = 90, 63 + 27 = 90,
24 + 66 = 90. They are all multiples of 10.
95 + 5 = 100, 23 + 77 = 100, 60 + 40 = 100. 98 + 2 = 100,
20 + 80 = 100, 88 + 12 = 100, 59 + 41 = 100, 51 + 49 = 100,
40 + 60 = 100, 48 + 52 = 100.

page 11
8 x 2 = 16, 45 ÷ 5 = 9, 6 x 5 = 30, 18 ÷ 2 = 9, 9 x 10 = 90, 50 ÷ 10 = 5,
5 x 3 = 15, 25 ÷ 5 = 5, 2 x 7 = 14, 60 ÷ 10 = 6, 23 x 10 = 230,
350 ÷ 10 = 35, 25 x 2 = 50, 34 ÷ 2 = 17, 30 x 10 = 300, 100 ÷ 2 = 50,
14 x 2 = 28, 650 ÷ 10 = 65, 3 x 100 = 300, 700 ÷ 100 = 7.

page 12
LEARNING THESE FACTS HELPS TO SOLVE
HARDER PROBLEMS

page 13
40 + 30 = 70, 50 + 90 = 140, 60 + 70 = 130, 70 + 80 = 150,
500 + 600 = 1100, 600 + 900 = 1500, 800 + 400 = 1200,
400 + 300 = 700, 60 − 10 = 50, 90 − 30 = 60, 80 − 40 = 40,
100 − 30 = 70, 600 − 400 = 200, 1200 − 300 = 900, 700 − 100 = 600,
1500 − 800 = 700.
60 = 100 − 40
80 = 30 + 50
500 = 900 − 400
800 = 1200 − 400
1400 = 600 + 800

page 14
Ring: 3 + 7, 6 + 4, 5 + 5, 2 + 8
Ring: 40 + 60, 20 + 80, 30 + 70, 90 + 10
Ring: 38 + 62, 18 + 82, 53 + 47, 24 + 76
45 + 55, 56 + 44, 37 + 63, 81 + 19, 46 + 54, 34 + 66, 71 + 29

page 15
500, 300, 800, 50, 250, 350.
The hidden number is 74

page 16
20, 50, 200, 120, 51, 67, 100

page 17
11 r1, 7 r1, 6 r1, 13 r1, 6 r4, 8 r3, 9 r2, 8 r1, 6 r2
2 teams with 2 left over
5 boxes with 2 left over
4 crates with 5 left over

page 18
£3.50, £4.50, £2.50, £2.25, £3.50, £4.25, £3.20, £6.40, £9.75, £3.20,
£4.30, £6.40.
£3.20, £2.50, £2.50

page 19
4 x 4 to 10 x 4: 16, 20, 24, 28, 32, 36, 40
4 x 3 to 10 x 3: 12, 15, 18, 21, 24, 27, 30

page 20
7 x 2 = 14, 6 x 3 = 18, 8 x 4 = 32, 10 x 5 = 50, 9 x 10 = 90.
Pick key 15.

page 21
THE TREASURE IS HIDDEN FOUR TIMES SIX PACES NORTH
OF THE OLD STATUE.

page 22
4 x 3 = 12, then x 2 = 24,
5 x 3 = 15, then x 2 = 30,
6 x 3 = 18, then x 2 = 36,
7 x 3 = 21, then x 2 = 42,
8 x 3 = 24, then x 2 = 48,
9 x 3 = 27, then x 2 = 54,
10 x 3 = 30, then x 2 = 60.
6 x 11 = 60 + 6 = 66,
9 x 11 = 90 + 9 = 99,
11 x 11 = 110 + 11 = 121,
14 x 11 = 140 + 14 = 154,
15 x 11 = 150 + 15 = 165,
20 x 11 = 200 + 20 = 220,
19 x 11 = 190 + 19 = 209

page 23
6 x 9 = 54, 7 x 9 = 63, 9 x 9 = 81, 11 x 9 = 99, 15 x 9 = 135,
20 x 9 = 180, 25 x 9 = 225

page 24
13 x 10 to 80 x 10 = 130, 140, 150, 160, 170, 180, 190, 200.
400, 450, 500, 550, 600, 650, 700, 750, 800.
320, 240, 480, 530, 1350, 2460.
800, 1500, 2300, 5400, 6800, 12 500.

page 25
38 boxes, 47 boxes, I56 boxes, 260 boxes.
38 lorries, 29 lorries, 86 lorries, I00 lorries.

page 26
The correct answers are: $425 - 38 = 387$, $347 - 85 = 262$,
$531 - 143 = 388$.
$350 \div 5 = 70$, $156 \div 3 = 52$, $164 \div 4 = 41$

page 27
The first two and the last calculations are wrong.
$24 + 30 + 16 = 83$, $56 + 38 = 121$, $356 + 462 = 889$ are all wrong.

page 28

page 29

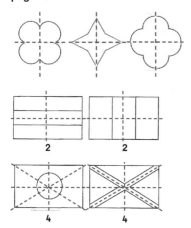

page 30
A E G C B F D H

page 31
A *square* has 4 sides and 4 right angles. 0 angle is larger than a right angle. 0 angle is smaller than a right angle. It has 4 vertices.
A *rectangle* has 4 sides and 4 right angles. 0 angle is larger than a right angle. 0 angle is smaller than a right angle. It has 4 vertices.
This *triangle* has 3 sides and 0 right angles. 0 angle is larger than a right angle. 3 angles are smaller than a right angle. It has 3 vertices.
A *circle* has 0 sides and 0 right angles. 0 angle is larger than a right angle. 0 angle is smaller than a right angle. It has 0 vertices.
A *parallelogram* has 4 sides and 0 right angles. 2 angles are larger than a right angle. 2 angles are smaller than a right angle. It has 4 vertices.

This *pentagon* has 5 sides and 0 right angles. 5 angles are larger than a right angle. 0 angle is smaller than a right angle. It has 5 vertices.
A *hexagon* has 6 sides and 0 right angles. 6 angles are larger than a right angle. 0 angle is smaller than a right angle. It has 6 vertices.
An *octagon* has 8 sides and 0 right angles. 8 angles are larger than a right angle. 0 angle is smaller than a right angle. It has 8 vertices.

page 32
A. Circle
B. Equilateral triangle
C. Semi-circle
D. Triangle
E. Square
F. Isosceles triangle
G. Pentagon
H. Quadrilateral
I. Rectangle
J. Hexagon
K. Heptagon
L. Regular hexagon

page 33
Cuboid 6, 12, 8
Triangular prism 5, 9, 6
Cube 6, 12, 8
Tetrahedron 4, 6, 4

page 34
I6cm
$8 \times 3cm = 24cm$; the hexagon is bigger, it has a perimeter of $6 \times 3cm = 18cm$
Use a ruler to measure each perimeter carefully.

page 35
A 8cm², **B** 12cm², **C** 2cm², **D** 15cm², **E** 12cm², **F** 10cm², **G** 16cm²

page 36
A 12cm, 8cm²
B 14cm, 12cm²
C 18cm, 14cm²
D 16cm, 7cm²
E 16cm, 16cm²
F 20cm, 24cm²

page 37
A 12cm, 6cm²
B 14cm, 10cm²
C 18cm, 11cm²
D 24cm, 15cm²
E 24cm, 22cm²
F 20cm, 16cm²

page 38
A 12cm³; **B** 18cm³; **C** 24cm³; **D** 40cm³; **E** 6cm³; **F** 32cm³

page 39
A 8cm³; **B** 4cm³; **C** 8cm³; **D** 12cm³· **E** 5cm³; **F** 9cm³; **G** 6cm³,
H 10cm³; **I** 13cm³

page 40
I measuring jug, ml
2 foot measure/ruler, cm
3 scales, g
4 tape measure, m/cm

page 41
km; m; kg; g; ml; g; cm or mm; mm; litre; mm

page 42

There are 100 centimetres in a metre; there are 50 centimetres in half a metre

75cm; 38cm; 134cm; 154cm; 98cm

1.42m; 1.54m; 1.98m; 0.98m; 1.34m

page 43

350cm = 3.5m

1.36m = 1 m 36cm

1m 5cm = 1.05m

7.02m = 7 metres 2cm

149cm = 1m 49cm

1m 54cm = 1.54m

0.95m = 95cm

950cm = 9.5m

1.5m = 150cm

page 44

500ml, 1000ml, 100ml

B, C

500ml, 250ml, 150ml, 900ml, 750ml, 850ml

page 45

$\frac{1}{4}$kg, $1\frac{3}{4}$kg, $2\frac{1}{2}$kg; $1\frac{1}{2}$kg; $2\frac{1}{4}$kg, $1\frac{3}{4}$kg

page 46

A 85mm

B 10.5cm

C 300ml

D 450ml

E 40kg

F 70kg

page 47

A 340cm; 150cm; 430cm; 340cm

B 50cm; 10cm; 600cm; 600cm

C 200g; 1200g; 4600g; 5800g

D 100g; 0g; 4300g; 1000g

page 48

Wednesday; 17 November; Yes, it is a week day; 6 December; 25 days; 24 October

page 49

Monster Trucks starts at 5:20; *Aussie Street* begins at 5:35; *Ward 7* lasts 40 minutes; *Cartoon Mystery* is 15 minutes longer than the *News*; 1 hour and 35 minutes longer.

Revenge of the Turtle: 4:00 pm to 5:29 pm

Haunted Castle IV: 6:00 pm to 7:58 pm

Mad for Maths III: 8 pm to 9:15 pm

page 50

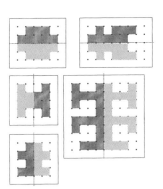

page 51

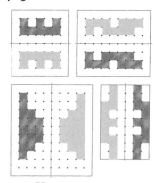

page 52

A $\frac{1}{2}$, half; B $\frac{1}{10}$, tenth; C $\frac{1}{5}$, fifth; D $\frac{1}{3}$, third; E $\frac{2}{3}$, two-thirds; F $\frac{1}{4}$, quarter

page 53

1 rectangle = $\frac{1}{10}$

10 rectangles = one whole

5 rectangles = $\frac{1}{2}$

2 rectangles = $\frac{1}{5}$

4 rectangles = $\frac{1}{3}$

8 rectangles = $\frac{2}{3}$

3 rectangles = $\frac{1}{4}$

page 54

A $\frac{7}{12}$; B $\frac{1}{4}$; C $\frac{5}{8}$; D $\frac{2}{5}$; E $\frac{1}{3}$; F $\frac{1}{6}$; G $\frac{3}{10}$; H $\frac{9}{20}$

page 55

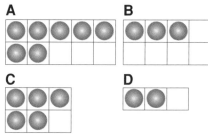

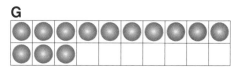

page 56

$\frac{1}{2}$ of 10 = 5; $\frac{1}{4}$ of 8 = 2; $\frac{1}{10}$ of 10 = 1; $\frac{1}{3}$ of 9 = 3

To find $\frac{1}{2}$, divide by 2; to find $\frac{1}{3}$, divide by 3; to find $\frac{1}{4}$, divide by 4; to find $\frac{1}{10}$ divide by 10

page 57

$\frac{1}{2}$: the circle has been cut into 2 pieces and we have I

$\frac{1}{3}$: the circle has been cut into 3 pieces and we have I

$\frac{1}{4}$: the circle has been cut into 4 pieces and we have I

$\frac{2}{3}$: the circle has been cut into 3 pieces and we have 2

$\frac{3}{4}$: the circle has been cut into 4 pieces and we have 3

page 58

A $\frac{1}{4} \to \frac{3}{4}$ $\frac{1}{6} \to \frac{5}{6}$ $\frac{1}{2} \to \frac{1}{2}$

$\frac{1}{3} \to \frac{2}{3}$ $\frac{1}{5} \to \frac{4}{5}$ $\frac{1}{8} \to \frac{7}{8}$

B $\frac{3}{10} \to \frac{7}{10}$ $\frac{5}{8} \to \frac{3}{8}$ $\frac{2}{5} \to \frac{3}{5}$

$\frac{4}{7} \to \frac{3}{7}$ $\frac{2}{7} \to \frac{5}{7}$ $\frac{4}{9} \to \frac{5}{9}$

C $\frac{3}{10} \to \frac{7}{10}$ $\frac{5}{10} \to \frac{5}{10}$ $\frac{9}{10} \to \frac{1}{10}$

$\frac{8}{10} \to \frac{2}{10}$ $\frac{6}{10} \to \frac{4}{10}$ $\frac{7}{10} \to \frac{3}{10}$

page 59

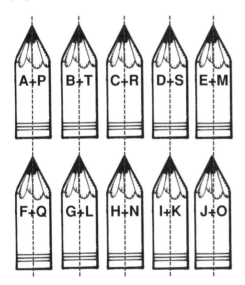

page 60

Cleaning the car: £3 each

Walking the dog: £1 each

Cleaning the kitchen: £4 each

Cleaning the windows: £9

9; 6; 3; 5

page 6I

$\frac{1}{4}$, 3; $\frac{1}{3}$, 4; $\frac{1}{10}$, 2, divide 20 by I0

page 62

A smallest, middle, largest

B middle, largest, smallest

C middle, smallest, largest

page 63

A ✗; B ✔; C ✔; D ✔; E ✔; F ✗; G ✔; H ✗; I ✗; J ✗; K ✗; L ✔;

M ✔; N ✔; O ✗; P ✔; Q ✔; R ✗; S ✗; T ✗; U ✔; V ✔; W ✔; X ✔

page 64

A 6, $\frac{1}{6}$; B 8, $\frac{1}{8}$; C 4, $\frac{1}{4}$; D 3, $\frac{1}{3}$

page 65

A Each person has 4 equal pieces

B Each person has 2 equal pieces

C Each person has 8 equal pieces

D Each person has I piece

page 66

A 2, 3; B 4, 6; C I0, I5

page 67

A   I tube – I0 sweets

2 tubes – 20 sweets

3 tubes – 30 sweets

4 tubes – 40 sweets

5 tubes – 50 sweets

B   I plate – 5 cookies

2 plates – I0 cookies

3 plates – I5 cookies

4 plates – 20 cookies

5 plates – 25 cookies

C   2 pieces – I extra

4 pieces – 2 extra

6 pieces – 3 extra

8 pieces – 4 extra

I0 pieces – 5 extra

D   4 tokens – I monster

8 tokens – 2 monsters

I2 tokens – 3 monsters

I6 tokens – 4 monsters

20 tokens – 5 monsters

page 68

A $\frac{2}{3}$; B $\frac{1}{6}$; C $\frac{4}{9}$; D $\frac{6}{14}$ *or* $\frac{3}{7}$; E $\frac{3}{5}$; F $\frac{2}{6}$ *or* $\frac{1}{3}$; G $\frac{3}{4}$; H $\frac{2}{4}$ *or* $\frac{1}{2}$

page 69

A $\frac{6}{25}$; B $\frac{6}{36}$ *or* $\frac{1}{6}$; C $\frac{5}{25}$ *or* $\frac{1}{5}$, D $\frac{5}{50}$ *or* $\frac{1}{10}$

page 70

250ml, $\frac{1}{4}$

A $\frac{1}{2}$, 500ml; B $\frac{1}{4}$, 500ml; C $\frac{1}{2}$, I500ml

I0 cups hold I litre, so 30 cups hold 3 litres

I litre fills 4 bowls, so 4 litres fill I6 bowls

about $\frac{1}{4}$ the children will get custard

page 7I

A I000m ÷ 2 = 500m

B 500m + 750m = I250m

C I250m + 750m = 2000m

25cm is $\frac{1}{4}$ of I metre

50cm is $\frac{1}{2}$ of I metre

page 72
A £5.20, £5.84, £6.25, £6.90, £7.65
B £1.25, £1.68, £2.14, £2.41, £2.56

page 73
A Mark (£4.20), James (£3.64),
   Mary (£3.25), Jenny (£2.98),
   Robin (£2.18), Rosie (£1.63)
B Carolyn (£4.52), Ben (£4.25),
   Alan (£3.49), Anne (£2.99),
   Colin (£2.36), Barbara (£2.15)

page 74
A $\frac{1}{4}$ 0.25
B $\frac{1}{2}$ 0.5
C $\frac{3}{4}$ 0.75
D $\frac{1}{2}$ 0.5
E I whole
F $\frac{1}{4}$ 0.25
G $\frac{3}{4}$ 0.75
H $\frac{1}{2}$ 0.5
I $\frac{1}{2}$ 0.5

page 75
$\frac{2}{10}$ 0.2; $\frac{3}{10}$ 0.3; $\frac{4}{10}$ 0.4; $\frac{9}{10}$ 0.9; $\frac{6}{10}$ 0.6; $\frac{8}{10}$ 0.8; $\frac{7}{10}$ 0.7; $\frac{1}{10}$ 0.1; $\frac{5}{10}$ or $\frac{1}{2}$ 0.5.

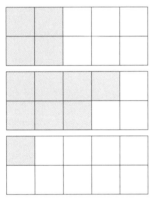

page 76
Answers from left to right: 7, 6, 15, 25, 4, 55, 10, 5, 3, 7, 6, 25, 8, 20, 80, 100, +, +, +, +, −, −, −, −

page 77
3 and 9, 3 and 5, 47, 24, 8, 8 and 16, 2 and 7, 14 and 7; 0, 5

page 78
The magic squares are I and 5

page 79
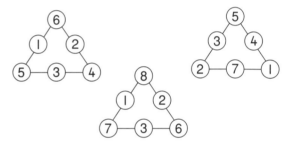
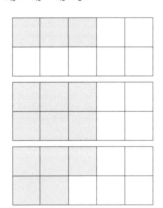

page 80
5 and 8, 7 and 5, 2 and 9, 6 and 8

page 81
6, 7 and 8; 15, 16 and 17; 7, 9 and 11; 16, 18, and 20

page 82
25 + 9 = 34, 35 − 14 = 21,
13 + 16 = 29, 36 − 12 = 24.
Various answers are possible, e.g., 33 + 3 = 36, 43 − 5 = 38,
35 + 17 = 52, 45 − 26 = 19

page 83
Various combinations are possible, e.g.,
2, 3, 5, 8 and 1, 4, 6, 7;
2, 3, 6, 7 and 1, 4, 5, 8
Various combinations are possible, e.g.,
9, 4, 2 and 8, 6, 1 and 3, 5, 7;
8, 3, 4 and 9, 5, 1 and 7, 6, 2

page 84   **page 85**

page 86
8 triangles, square-based pyramid, triangular prism

page 87
cube, cylinder, rectangular prism, hemisphere. A triangular prism has three faces that are rectangles and two identical triangular ends.

page 88
16 articles, 2 articles on each page, 240 sheets, 6 minutes

page 89
£30.00, 25 copies are unsold, £17.50, £9.50

page 90
Granny £5.00; Uncle £2.50; Friend £1.00; Dad 10p per length; total £13.50

page 91
5 x £2 = £10.00
20 x £1 = £20.00
10 x 50p = £5.00
10 x 20p = £2.00
20 x 10p = £2.00
20 x 5p = £1.00
50 x 2p = £1.00
100 x 1p = £1.00
Total £42.00
5 x £2 = 2 x £5 notes
20 x £1 = 2 x £10 notes
10 x 50p = 1 x £5 note
10 x 20p = 2 x £1 coins
20 x 10p = 2 x £1 coins
20 x 5p = 1 x £1 coin
50 x 2p = 1 x £1 coin
100 x 1p = 1 x £1 coin

page 92
£4.80, £17.75, £2.25, two 2 litre bottles are cheaper by 50p

page 93
£1.50 + £1.20 + £2.50 + 75p + 90p = £6.85. £3.15 change

page 94
20 x 5kg = 100kg, 6 or 7 apples in each bag, 20 bags, 40 bottles

page 95
potatoes 3kg, lemonade 1 litre or 2 litres, sugar 1kg; ribbon 25m, milk 1 litre or 2 litres, shoelaces 45cm

page 96
Tuesday, Thursday, 31, Thursday, 24 January, Friday, Friday

page 97
Gym Display, School Band, Gym Display, 20 minutes, 9.15 p m

page 98
6.00, 45 minutes, 50 minutes, 1 hour and 50 minutes, One Man and His Pig, Queen Street, Star Trip, 1 hour

page 99
8.15 am, 9.00 am, 45 minutes, 10 minutes, 9.10 am, 3 hours and 5 minutes, 2.15 pm, yes at 3.12 pm.

page 100
Joe brought 30 cakes, Tina brought 28 scones, Jack brought 25, 3 less than Tina. Yes, there were 20 + 40 + 45 = 105 chairs

page 101
Mary made £2.40, Jane made £3.00, Mike brought 63 sandwiches altogether. Carla bought apple tarts: £1.00 – 10p = 90p; 90 ÷ 6 = 15p

page 102
120 boys, 30 boys like football, 40 girls like football, one-quarter

page 103
One-quarter use blue ropes, half prefer the climbing frame, one-third prefer the scramble net. 12 prefer a longer playtime, two-fifths eat fruit.

page 104

+	1	2	3	4	5	6	7	8	9	10
1	2	3	4	5	6	7	8	9	10	11
2	3	4	5	6	7	8	9	10	11	12
3	4	5	6	7	8	9	10	11	12	13
4	5	6	7	8	9	10	11	12	13	14
5	6	7	8	9	10	11	12	13	14	15
6	7	8	9	10	11	12	13	14	15	16
7	8	9	10	11	12	13	14	15	16	17
8	9	10	11	12	13	14	15	16	17	18
9	10	11	12	13	14	15	16	17	18	19
10	11	12	13	14	15	16	17	18	19	20

Answer	Frequency
1–4	6
5–8	22
9–12	36
13–16	26
17–20	10

9–12 because all the numbers are part of a number bond that makes 9–12; 1–4 because they are small numbers, there are not many number bonds that make 1–4; 1 does not appear in the answers because the lowest addition is 1 + 1 = 2

page 105

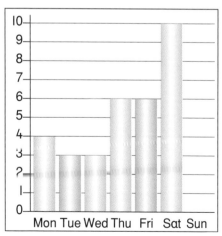

Saturday; 10; Sunday because no TVs were sold; 18

page 106
12, 6, 25, 17; lorry = 1, car = 3, motorbike = 2; total = 6

page 107
fish = ⊞ II; starfish = ⊞ I; octopus = II; sea snail = ⊞ ⊞ III
house = ⊞ III; chimney-pot = ⊞ ⊞ II; window = ⊞ ⊞ ⊞ I;
door = ⊞ III

page 108

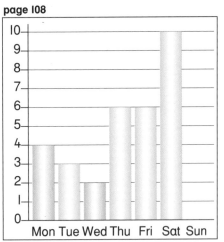

The first Thursday and the second Sunday because they watched lots of TV. The family went out on the first Sunday because no TV was watched. The family watched most TV in week I

page 109

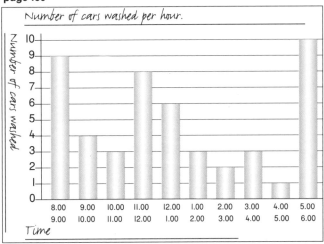

page 110

Morning and evening; it is when people are travelling to and from school and work

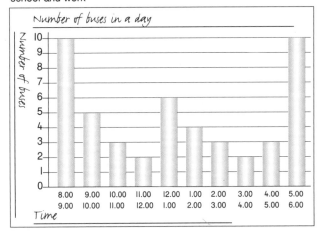

page III

9; Mon = 9, Tues = 12; Wed = 7; Thu = 6; Fri = 5; Sat = 8; Sun = 10
Tuesday; Thursday; Friday

page 112

30; 5; 15. Jan = 30; Feb = 20; Mar = 65; Apr = 10; May = 20;
Jun = 5; Jul = 35; Aug = 55; Sep = 45; Oct = 15; Nov = 5; Dec = 25

page 113

January = $2\frac{1}{4}$ pictograms; February = $1\frac{3}{4}$; March = $1\frac{1}{2}$; April = $1\frac{1}{4}$;
May = 1; June = 1; July = $\frac{1}{2}$; August = 0; September = 2; October = $2\frac{1}{2}$;
November = $2\frac{3}{4}$; December = $3\frac{1}{4}$.
The weather is colder; August because no hot dinners were sold; pictograms can be clearer because there is less counting but you may have other reasons

page 114

60 crossings = 3 pictograms; 100 = 5; 120 = 6; 140 = 7; 160 = 8;
180 = 9; 15 = $\frac{3}{4}$; 25 = $1\frac{1}{4}$; 40 = 2; 110 = $5\frac{1}{2}$

page 115

Jan = 20, Feb = 45, March = 65, April = 50, May = 70, June = 80,
July = 95, Aug = 100, Sept = 80, Oct = 75, Nov = 60, Dec = 15.
December; August; April; June and September

page 116

Intervals of 5 or 10

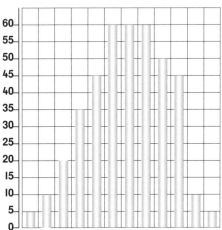

page 117

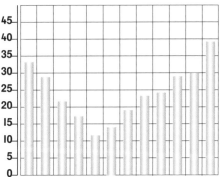

Christmas and the New Year sales.

page 118

soaps; 4: cartoons, dramas, soaps, films; horror; films; dramas; soaps because they have the most viewers

page 119

nut roast; nut roast 11:55; potatoes 12:20; gravy 12:55; carrots 12:50; sprouts 12:40; peas 12:45; roast potatoes 12:10

page 121

Computer games and swimming are most popular; watching TV least